END OF FERN CANYON

THE BEST OF
REMINISCE

CONTENTS

REMINISCE

ASSOCIATE CREATIVE DIRECTOR:
Christina Spalatin
DEPUTY EDITOR: Linda Kast
ASSOCIATE EDITOR: Julie Kuczynski
LAYOUT DESIGNERS: Sabine Beaupre,
Payton Hintz
SENIOR COPY EDITOR: Dulcie Shoener
PRODUCTION ARTIST: Jill Banks
SENIOR RIGHTS ASSOCIATE: Jill Godsey

PICTURED ON FRONT COVER:
Playing London Bridge on page 25,
Joan Brandy
Leather, Strannik_fox/Shutterstock

PICTURED ON BACK COVER:
Car passengers on page 140,
Mark Steffen
Prom couple on page 61,
Cecilia Ann Francis
Serviceman on page 122, Weldon Reese

ADDITIONAL PHOTO CREDIT:
Vintage scrapbook page,
OHishiapply/Shutterstock

© 2019 RDA Enthusiast Brands, LLC.
1610 N. 2nd St., Suite 102
Milwaukee, WI 53212-3906

International Standard Book Number:
978-1-61765-846-4
International Standard Serial Number:
Applied for
Component Number: 117300062H

SINGLE FILE

These children of the 1960s cross the street in front of their school in an orderly fashion with the assistance of a very official-looking crossing guard. If only the dairy truck were an ice cream truck.

LARRY STEVENS · HATFIELD, PA

Take a walk down memory lane with us. We've selected the best of the best stories, photos and memories from the previous year of *Reminisce* magazine and compiled them here for you to enjoy and share with generations to come. There's something of interest for everyone!

The Best of Reminisce highlights the innocence of youth, fond memories of families with terrific photos from keepsake albums, and the excitement of true love. You'll also find some good ol'-fashioned fun, accounts of hard work by everyday people, stories of courageous animals during war years, Route 66 nostalgia, chance encounters with stars such as Mel Torme, and special holiday traditions with loved ones. Finally, laugh out loud at the antics in the last chapter, and get a kick out of large, colorful vintage ads sprinkled throughout the book.

Discover heartwarming happiness and so much more with *The Best of Reminisce*.

THE EDITORS OF *REMINISCE* MAGAZINE

CHAPTER 1

GROWING UP

Ah, to be a kid again! Experience the joys and follies of youth with thoughtful memories and fun photos from the past.

Hoops Pride

The Republic High School boys basketball team brought home its first
Class M State Championship in March 1963 with a win
at the University of Missouri–Columbia.

CINDY BROWN · SPRINGFIELD, MO

No Bush League Instructor

Mom was simply a natural at playing second base.

Mothers are complicated creatures. I found that out at 12 in 1950 when I had my first opportunity to play organized baseball. Our church, Caldwell Memorial Presbyterian, had decided to field a youth baseball team. We played other teams in the Charlotte, North Carolina, area.

Our uniforms were gray trimmed in blue with Caldwell on the front and our numbers on the back. I was number 10. I wore my blue cap everywhere and bought cleats with the money I earned delivering newspapers. I was excited to learn, but little did I know what I'd learn from my mother that summer.

The coaching staff found out rather quickly that I played infield better than I played outfield. They tried me at second base, but after the second practice I went home with dirt up my backside and my spirits lower than the spikes of my cleats. On every play, I was knocked flat.

As I got off my bicycle, my mom came out onto the porch. She took one good look at my dirty clothes and the expression on my face and asked, "What happened?"

After I told her, she put down her dish towel, came out to the yard, took my glove and showed

Harry's mom, Dessie, loved three things: her family, her church and her flower garden.

me how to play second base. She showed me how to crouch on the balls of my feet with the glove low and ready for a ground ball. She showed me footwork and how to handle an aggressive base runner.

The idea had never crossed my mind that my mom had played ball. So I watched, listened and practiced the footwork. There was more to this than I thought.

Then she sat down on the porch steps and told me a secret. She'd grown up in Indian Trail, North Carolina, and played second base for the high school girls softball team.

One day the boys baseball team played a game with the girls team. One boy tried to turn a single into a double and roared down the baseline toward the girl between him and the bag. My mother, the girl, decked him. From then on, everyone called her Deck. She never told anyone the story about her nickname because it wasn't ladylike to do such things.

I kept her secret safely locked in my heart until she passed away. When I revealed the story at her funeral, it brought smiles to many faces having a hard time trying to smile that day.

HARRY L. RAST JR. · NORTH CHESTERFIELD, VA

WHAT A CATCH!

OUR DAUGHTER CATHERINE, 8, joined the spring fishing derby at Kirk's Pond in Oxford, Connecticut, in 1972. It was raining that day and she had a pole with no reel—only a line and a hook.

Most of the other anglers fished from the opposite side of the pond, but Catherine wanted to be close to me because I was in charge of hot chocolate and doughnuts.

After fishing patiently for quite some time, Catherine screamed with excitement and pulled a big fish out of the water. In fact, she caught the largest fish of the day, and for her efforts she won a fishing pole and spinning reel.

To top it all off, a picture of her with her big catch made the front page of the local newspaper.

PATRICIA CROWTHER
EDGEWATER, FL

Catherine holds her prizewinning fish for the camera.

THE SWING IN THE CELLAR

OUR SMALL ROW HOUSE HAD barely enough room for living, let alone for three children to play. We went outdoors when weather permitted, but if snow, rain and cold kept us indoors, we were stumped. Thankfully, my mother had a plan. Our cellar, she mused, would make the perfect playroom. The heat from the coal furnace would provide a warm refuge from the cold city street, and with a few inexpensive improvements, Mother was sure it could work.

She took an old woolen rug and covered the floor in the new playroom. She added two floor lamps and hung a curtain in front of some storage shelves. She placed our bookcase and toy box along the wall. But the main attraction was yet to come.

She sent us to the hardware store to buy four thick metal bolts and a large coil of heavy rope. My father attached the bolts to the ceiling rafters, then used the rope and some thick boards to make two indoor swings.

The playroom quickly became a neighborhood sensation. When Mother offered homemade oatmeal cookies and milk, the playroom was hard to leave, no matter the weather outside.

DOROTHY STANAITIS
GLOUCESTER CITY, NJ

Dorothy holds hands with younger friends in front of the decorative grills that opened to deliver coal to her basement.

A Bar Too High

When the coach takes a tumble.

———

Growing up in Floral, Arkansas, in the late '50s and through the '60s, I spent most of my time playing outdoors.

In those days, kids rode bicycles and climbed on trees, rocks or playground equipment. Spending time inside occurred mostly in winter when it was too cold to stay outside very long.

One summer around 1961 my parents bought me a metal swing set. I remember the day we received the big box of multicolored metal bars. My Uncle Emmett put the bars together to form the most beautiful, modern swing set I had ever seen.

I was so excited! I loved it and spent time on it every day. The set was such a grand improvement from the old rope swing I was used to, and I played on the slide, teeter totter or swing all the time.

When my cousin Teresa came over, the two of us played on it together. I was tall for my age and could jump up and reach the top bar and turn flips. Teresa was shorter than me and unable to master that feat. But because I believed I was such a brilliant gymnast, I decided to teach her how to catch the high bar and do flips, too.

In hindsight, she probably couldn't have reached the bar anyway, but I was determined that I could teach her.

"Do exactly like I do!" I said, convinced that I really was a star. I ran, took a giant leap, missed the bar completely, and landed flat on my back. Then, being in shock, I took a deep breath, but no air would enter my lungs. I lay there, gasping to breathe.

For the first time in my life I understood what the phrase "knocked the wind out of me" meant. I guess you could say my attempt to catch the high bar had left me totally breathless and grounded. The whole time, Teresa just stood there staring at me in amazement and fear. At that point, she was determined not to do *exactly* as I did!

ANGELINE BROWN STONER
FLORAL, AR

My attempt to catch the high bar left me breathless and grounded.

Angeline's new swing set delivered hours of outdoor fun.

Fistful of Pennies

A short bike ride turns into sweet satisfaction.

Whenever my mind wanders and someone offers "a penny for your thoughts," I grin and think about a special place in Hilbert, Wisconsin. For those of us lucky enough to have grown up there in the 1960s and '70s, we had only to bike up Main Street to find the best spot in town—Krautkramer General Store.

It's 1968 and I'm a carefree, freckle-faced 8-year-old. St. Mary's is closed for the summer, and Mom has just brushed my hair into high pigtails and swabbed my sister Toby's knee with Mercurochrome.

She hands me a $5 bill and tells us to go to Krautkramer's for groceries. I ask if we can keep the change. (You see, Krautkramer's has the ultimate penny candy counter.) Mom nods and dries her hands on her apron.

With the money tucked in my pocket, Toby and I pedal off to the store. I pick up a loaf of Wonder Bread, summer sausage, stinky cheese and a six-pack of Fresca. Mrs. Krautkramer punches numbers into the big black cash register while her husband wraps the sausage before sliding it into our brown paper bag.

"Twelve cents back, dearie," says Mrs. K as she drops a dozen shiny pennies into my sweaty palm.

"Mom said we can get penny candy if there's change left," I tell her.

I got an A in second-grade math, so to be fair, Toby gets six pennies and I get six pennies.

"Wow, we're rich," Toby beams. Ten minutes later, Mrs. K drops our sweet treasures into two tiny brown bags and we plop our pennies onto the scratched wooden counter.

Skipping out the door, I see Mr. K hand a blue bottle of Windex and a roll of paper towels to his wife so she can get the candy counter ready for the next freckle-faced boy or girl who arrives with a fistful of pennies.

DARLENE BUECHEL · CHILTON, WI

Too Good Not to Share

A teenage boy, a disabled old woman and the special dog they both loved.

———

When I was growing up on the south side of Chicago in the 1950s, I had a pet collie named Lady. For nine years, Lady and I were inseparable and, at 14, I loved her with all my heart.

She had uncanny intelligence and instinct. She'd saved my little brother Ricky's life when he'd toddled into an alley just as a large truck was turning into the lane. Lady quickly ran to Ricky and pinned him up against a fence until the truck passed.

One day I went to do my paper route, leaving Lady in our yard as usual. Unfortunately, I forgot to lock the gate and she got out.

When I realized she was gone, I was devastated. For weeks, I searched high and low for her, to no avail. I had to resign myself to never seeing her again. My sorrow almost overwhelmed me.

Yet a few months later, while riding in my cousin's car several blocks from my house, I saw a man walking a dog that looked a lot like Lady.

"Stop the car!" I shouted. "That's my dog!"

I spoke to the man, who told me that the dog was his mother's; she'd had her for several months. He looked doubtful when I told him she was mine, so I turned to her and said, "Lady, come." She immediately sat next to me in the heel position.

"It appears she is your dog," said the man, who had found her wandering around his neighborhood and had taken her in. I was eager to get her home, so I agreed to go with him to break the news to his mother.

When we got to the house, Lady ran directly to the man's mother, who was in a wheelchair.

Lady had been the woman's constant companion since they'd found her, the son said, and had done wonders for his mother's attitude and life outlook.

It was clear by the way she sat so faithfully at the woman's side that Lady had bonded with her.

When the woman learned I was there to reclaim my lost dog, she began to cry. Her son, who was also now crying, apologized but insisted that they give Lady back to me.

By this time tears were streaming down my cheeks, too. I was faced with a terrible dilemma. I loved my dog and wanted her back, but I realized there was no way that I could take her away from this elderly woman who badly needed Lady's companionship. It would be selfish.

I told the woman she could keep Lady.

She and her son were full of gratitude and promised me that I could visit Lady whenever I wanted. But I knew that would only bring me more heartache. I knew, too, it was best for everyone that I stay away. Lady was performing an essential service now; she and her new owner deserved a clean break, without the worry that in a moment of longing I would demand my dog back.

Choosing to allow Lady to stay there was without doubt the most difficult decision I'd had to make up to that point in my life—and it was one of the toughest decisions I've ever made.

My tears flow once more as I write. I never saw Lady again, but I take comfort knowing that this incident helped to form my character, and that my cherished pet made the remaining years of that sweet old woman's life better.

MICHAEL STECZO · MILLIKEN, CO

There was no way that I could take her away from this elderly woman who badly needed Lady's companionship.

Lady smiles as Michael's beloved pet. She later brightened the world of a new owner.

The Spy Chasers at Summer Camp

A lonely cottage, mysterious lights
and five very active imaginations.

When I was 10, I spent eight weeks at Camp Wahconah, a summer camp for girls near Pittsfield, Massachusetts. I didn't like it very much. It was too regimented, too competitive and too focused on athletics. But I did like the four girls with whom I shared a bunk and an unexpected adventure.

Our sleeping area was at the rear of the camp. Behind us were woods and, beyond the trees, an isolated summer cottage.

At night I watched the house from my bunk and noticed lights repeatedly going on, then off, briefly illuminating each window. I also saw what looked like a flashlight being clicked on and off in suspicious patterns.

I should add, this was 1943 and we were at war. There were rumors about German spies living in New York City and U-boats off the coast of Cape Cod. My young head was full of fears of evildoers and espionage.

One night, I told my four bunkmates of my worries. They quickly agreed the situation needed our careful attention. Appointing ourselves junior FBI agents, we'd slip out during rest hours and, using tree trunks for cover, spy on the "house of spies." We were convinced the light patterns were coded messages. We tried to decipher them but the code was complex.

Each time we ventured into the woods, we moved closer to the house. "We need a better look at the spies so we'll be able to identify them on wanted lists," I said. We even hatched a plan for two of us to knock on the door and claim to be lost, but we were too scared to carry it out.

One day in late August, we got caught in a downpour while maintaining our vigil. We decided to build a covering to protect us from the weather. We found a flat area free of tree roots, dug a large trench, stuck some branches into the ground and covered them with a piece of discarded linoleum.

The next time we arrived at the lean-to to watch our Nazis— for that's how we thought of them—we sniffed something foul. We had accidentally dug into a cesspool. That put a smelly end to our surveillance.

Soon after, it was time to go home. We never told anyone about the Nancy Drew Spycatchers Society of Bunk 12. But to this day I look back on it with astonishment and fondness. We'd turned an otherwise ordinary summer into something intoxicating, exciting and totally ours.

I wonder if the innocent vacationers staying in that house ever knew that they'd given us such a memorable experience?

At 10, Edith had a grand smile
and a yen for intrigue.

EDITH SAMUELS
CINCINNATI, OH

*We were convinced the light patterns
were coded messages.*

WHAT KIDS WANT

Colorful illustrations of smiling children helped to promote products for kids.

1958 »

Sips in Summer

This Libby's ad is aimed squarely at busy moms whose kids spend their summer days working up a thirst running from one naughty prank to another. The "frozen" beneath the bright red Libby's logo is almost an afterthought—and why not? Who has time to wait for fresh-squeezed juice when there's a baby sister to tease?

« 1955

Coonskin Craze

Kids went wild for coonskin caps after *Davy Crockett* debuted on ABC-TV in 1954. Soon the caps were showing up in dozens of product ads, such as this one from 1955 for Karo syrup.

Schooltime vs. Summertime

During one's youth, the year is divided into two seasons.

G rowing up in Sycamore, Illinois, in the early 1950s was like growing up in Mayberry. The town's charm was as much a function of the times as it was the place. Although the Korean War was underway, those sights and sounds didn't invade our homes every night the way Vietnam did.

As teenagers, we had scant experience with class distinctions, racial injustice, unemployment or poverty. Maybe we were naive living in the American heartland, sheltered from the harsh realities of the world. Regardless, it was really a wonderful time to be a teenager, and Sycamore was the best place to live.

As in most small towns, schools were the center of community activity. We respected our teachers and they cared about us. In those days, a call from the school to a parent about a child's behavior or bad grades was taken seriously.

To be expelled was the worst. Yet, I recall one threatened expulsion that, in hindsight, seems unfair. John, a fine student and a solid citizen, was sent home for wearing sideburns. Remember, this was before Elvis or the Beatles were popular. John soon shaved his sideburns and returned to school.

Teen Town, Sycamore's recreation and social center, was established in 1953. Membership cost only a nominal fee, and the center was open several nights a week. We went there to dance, play Ping-Pong or hang out.

Few of us had jobs after school, but many young women I knew worked as carhops at the drive-in restaurants. The drive-in was another excuse to socialize, a place where boys and girls met, where friendships and romances bloomed.

During the summer, I detasseled corn for The Ag, the DeKalb Agricultural Association. The job lasted only a few weeks, but it was a quick way to make money for clothes and supplies for the upcoming school year. It also laid the foundation for my strong work ethic.

Summer was when I learned to play golf. If you lived in the Sycamore Park District, you could play rounds for free on Tuesday and Thursday mornings. After a few friends and I found some old golf clubs, we played there often.

If you or a parent worked for the Anaconda Wire and Cable Co., the park's outdoor pool was free, too. My sisters and I often hopped on our bicycles and rode there to swim for the entire afternoon.

The city's welcome sign once read "Life Offers More in Sycamore." It did in the '50s; maybe it's still true today.

GENE BEHLER
INDIANAPOLIS, IN

MOM MADE IT HAPPEN

My father died when I was young, so when my mom came up with $48 for my senior class cruise on Lake Huron in 1954, I remember thinking how lucky I was. No matter the circumstances, my mother always came through for me. The SS *South American* was prepped for its first cruise of the tourist season, leaving from Detroit, Michigan, for Mackinac Island in Lake Huron and Canada's Sault Ste. Marie Locks that lead into Lake Superior. The three-day cruise was a perk for graduating from high school in Michigan in the early 1950s and was limited to 500 seniors.

JOHN LESJACK · SANTA ROSA, CA

1. On their senior class cruise in May 1954, clockwise from upper left, John Lesjack, Jim Everett, Chuck Peters and John Fow sit on the top deck of the ship. Tom O'Conner was the photographer. **2.** Seniors from East Detroit High School gather around the deck chairs. **3.** Friends since ninth grade, the self-styled Rugged Women of East Detroit High pose in front of a surrey while exploring Mackinac Island.

Strength of Spirit

Weighed down by braces on her legs, she stood taller than them all.

T he first day of second grade in 1952 was the scariest of my entire life. We had just moved to South Carolina for my dad's job and we were living in a Spartan Mansion trailer instead of a house. I knew no one, not even my teacher.

When I walked into the classroom, a bit late, everything was in order. Mrs. Gattis had stacked each desk with books, our names on top. We were instructed to copy and take home the notes that covered the blackboard.

As May Day king of second grade, Lester escorts his queen, Diane, at their school in Jackson, South Carolina. A friendship rekindled once Lester and Diane connected and they could rehash their past (top right).

I took my seat, second row, third back, and I noticed an empty desk at the end of my row. Everyone was silently writing as I started my own copying from the board.

That's when it began. I heard and felt an odd *thump, thump,* rhythmic, like a metronome from music class.

The sound gradually got louder; the vibrations stronger. Distracted, I stopped and looked at the door. It was closed. Everyone else, including my teacher, took no notice. Then the noise stopped and the heavy oak door flung open so hard it hit the wall.

In came a tiny blond girl in a pink dress teetering on one stiff leg at a time. She walked by swinging her upper body back and forth. Strangely, whenever her foot hit the floor, a loud thump would emanate as if a sledgehammer had struck.

Later I learned she had a belt around her waist attached to iron bars that ran down the sides of each leg, connected by an iron bar under each foot. A polio survivor, she had no strength in her legs.

She started moving slowly down the row to my left. She hit each desk as she went by but the kids didn't react, just rearranged their disheveled books and kept writing. They all knew her.

As she got close, a boy in the next row slid his foot under hers without looking up or giving any clue as to his intent. It worked. The girl tripped and fell forward like a tree felled in the woods; her knees didn't bend. She desperately grabbed at the empty desk as she hit the floor, her books scattering.

I went from frightened to furious. I leaped to my feet and drew back; I wanted to hit the boy. I glanced at Mrs. Gattis, expecting a reaction. She sat oblivious, nose in her paperwork.

Surprised, I bent to help the girl. She shot me a furious look, her face

*Diane sped down the long hallway
on roller skates, hair and dress flying.
She zipped by in a rainfall of giggles.*

contorted. "I'll do it myself!" she hissed. I stood as she pulled herself up, leaned her back against the wall, compressed her dress around a knee and clicked the trip release on her braces. Then, grabbing her desk, in a quick motion she swung her heinie and sat down hard. I picked up her books and clumsily arranged them on her desk. With a deep frown, she muttered, "Thanks."

In time, Diane and I became friends. I admired the way she fought through her days with little or preferably no help. When her face was not contorted, she was beautiful. I often forgot about the braces. But I could not forget how my teacher never stepped in to help. I was mad, angry at her; I just couldn't understand.

Some time later my mom told me that we were invited to Diane's house. We pulled up to the new ranch-style home. The front door opened and Diane's mom gestured us in. The biggest surprise came when I realized that in the doorway hugging my mom was Mrs. Gattis. My teacher was Diane's mom.

We walked into the kitchen and I noticed that the new cabinets were dented all along the bottom. Then I heard the sound of ball bearings spinning. Diane sped down the long hallway on roller skates, hair and dress flying. She zipped by in a rainfall of giggles.

When she got to the kitchen cabinets, Diane caught herself with her hands, but she had no control over her feet. The heavy metal braces added momentum as her shoes splintered across the wood cabinets, fitting perfectly into the cabinetry indentations.

Mrs. Gattis paid no attention. She smiled, drank coffee and continued conversing with my mom. I then suddenly understood Mrs. Gattis and the classroom situation.

Diane's determination and courage at such a young age have always been an inspiration to me. I've told her story to people many times over the years.

My parents moved a lot when I was young, and Diane and I lost touch. Recently I found her using the internet and we reconnected after all these years.

LESTER BROOKSHIRE
ROME, GA

PRESSING FOR A CURE

Polio and its prevention riveted early 20th-century America.

1916
New York City records more than 2,300 polio-related deaths.

....

1921
At 39, Franklin Delano Roosevelt contracts polio.

....

1933
FDR is inaugurated as president.

....

1938
FDR launches the National Foundation for Infantile Paralysis, now the March of Dimes.

....

1946
President Truman declares nationwide war on polio.

....

1947
Dr. Jonas Salk is recruited to find a cure.

....

1952
A record 57,628 cases of polio are reported in the U.S.

....

1953
The Salk vaccine is developed for testing.

....

1954
In a massive field trial, nearly 2 million children are inoculated.

....

1955-'57
Polio rate falls by almost 90%.

....

1979
The polio virus is eliminated in the U.S.

KIDDING AROUND

My mother took this photo of my sister (left), younger brother and me in 1951. As you can see, it was windy that day on the farm in Kimball, South Dakota.

SUSAN ANN PIBAL · PIERRE, SD

LIKE GRANDPA
My father, Gabby Gebhardt, passes on his love of DIY to my son Jonathan in his New Jersey home's amazing workshop around 1986.
PHYLLIS GEBHARDT · KISSIMMEE, FL

THE COCK-A-DOODLE-DOO
My husband, Edward, raised chickens as a boy. Here he is during World War II with his favorite rooster, Tojo.
GWEN ASPLUNDH
HUNTINGDON VALLEY, PA

THE BATHING COMPANION

When I was a girl, I didn't play with dolls; I had my bantam chickens. This photo is from the mid-1940s when I was about 4. Whenever Mom gave me a bath, my little hen Bitsy would watch from her perch on the closed lid of the toilet.

JUDY PEARCE · CARPINTERIA, CA

KIDDING AROUND

Brenda and I have been friends since third grade, when her family moved to Westchester, New Hampshire. Here I am with Brenda (right) and her sister DeDe.

MARILYN MONS
MANCHESTER, NH

THAT'S MONKEY BUSINESS

My father-in-law, Donald Neilson, who lived in Los Angeles in 1939, told us about an organ grinder who would visit his neighborhood. When the kids heard him coming down the street, they would beg their parents for money, then hurry outside with their change. The man had a little monkey who ran around and collected money. Here, the monkey embraces Donald before returning to the organ grinder with the money.

JAMIE NEILSON
TRABUCO CANYON, CA

REACH FOR THE SKY

With shows like *The Lone Ranger* popular in the 1950s, it's no wonder my friends and I liked to play cowboys. I'm in the back with a pair of six-shooters.

RICK HNATH · NORTHVALE, NJ

ON STAGE

I was in fifth grade in McLean, Illinois, in 1947, when several one-room schools put on a joint musical. Based on the costumes, I think it was *Old King Cole*.

MARY NELSON · WEST LAFAYETTE, IN

KIDDING AROUND

GRIDIRON GOLIATHS
We were all-American kids, in sixth grade at Stanley Hall School in Evansville, Indiana, in 1963. From left, Jimmy Kappenman, Frank Johnson, Christopher Clayton and Eric Johnson; with the pigskin, Ernie Rogers and David Wilder.
REV. DAVID M. POLAND
LANSDALE, PA

❝

Shirley, 10, Valerie, 4, and Glenn, 5, pose after raiding the attic one day in 1967.

DORIS JOYCE · LACONIA, NH

❝

My cousin Arvid Miller and I were fishing in 1940 on Oak Lake, Minnesota, using tree branches for makeshift poles.

DOROTHY McCUNE
PARADISE, MT

MY FAIR LADY

I had endless fun playing London Bridge with my older sister Helen and our friend David in 1950. My grandma Rose Applebaum snapped the photo in Bliss Park in Brooklyn's Bay Ridge area.
JOAN BRANDY · BROOKLYN, NY

The Brauer boys, Chris, 10, and Ben, 8, captured in a rare filial embrace in the 1980s.

Wheel of Fortune

How a car tire set them on the course of their lives.

My younger brother Ben and I grew up across the street from a large park in a quiet neighborhood of Victoria, British Columbia. Our house was below street level, which meant that all groceries, camping gear, decorative rocks and anything else our parents made us haul had to be heaved up and down the steep front lawn, because the car was always parked on the road.

Like many children of the '80s, we spent Saturday mornings watching cartoons and enjoying sugary cereal. At some point before lunch, our mother would turn off the TV and shoo us outside.

One particular morning, she sent us to help our father change a car tire. Watching him get his hands dirty and swear under his breath was somehow considered male bonding. Eventually, he bestowed on us the responsibility of inching the old tire, rim and all, down the driveway and into the garage while he went inside.

It occurred to me that there might be a more efficient way to get the job done. An episode of *He-Man and the Masters of the Universe* was starting soon and I didn't want to miss it. My plan was to roll the heavy tire down the driveway and Ben would catch it. I didn't take physics or biology into consideration. I was just thinking about myself. And He-Man.

I sent Ben down to stand in the garage. I had him shuffle to the left and then a bit to the right until he was exactly at dead center. Then, closing one of my eyes to aim, I pushed the tire steadily into motion. I was quite proud of myself. As the thing picked up speed, I nodded in a self-congratulatory way.

Only when it neared the halfway mark did I suddenly realize that I might have been wrong. As the tire rolled faster and faster down its path of doom, with Ben standing there, arms outstretched like some sacrificial offering, I imagined the rest of my life as an only child.

Then something I can't explain happened. As the tire got closer to the garage it wobbled ever so slightly, changing direction. Rather than barreling into Ben, it hit the door next to the garage. In fact, it blew the door off its hinges.

Though I was relieved that my brother wasn't crushed, I knew the noise would bring our parents storming out, and Ben, who was 8, wasn't yet smart enough to lie. I was grounded. No *He-Man* or any other TV for a month.

I think of this incident with the tire as a defining moment for both of us. Ben is now an engineer and I bury myself in words as a writer. My brother chose to focus his life in the world of physics, and I chose to focus mine in the arts, where I can studiously avoid physics.

We haven't looked back since.

CHRIS BRAUER · CRESTON, BC

BOOKLETS OF LOVE
Vintage valentines from the 1940s certainly say it with charm.
I found these storybook-style cards among my parents' belongings.
Note the signature at the end: *Love, Precious Fuzzy Wuzzy.*
CAROL BYRON · EAST WILLIAMSON, NY

IN LOVE

THRILLING RIDE

In my senior year of high school in 1948, a friend asked me to a tobogganing party her mother was throwing for some local boys who'd helped her. They were all nice boys, but a red-haired, good-looking one named Wendell—Bunk, as he was known—caught my eye. Two years later, we married. That blind date on a toboggan made our future.
JOYCE GRUMMET · JENISON, MI

TRENDSETTING HUES

My mother, Ethel Blome, married my father, Charles Roedersheimer, on Nov. 21, 1940, a time of year when yellow flowers were the only fresh ones available. Her attendants were her sister Deloris in blue and my dad's sister Martha in pink. I think they wore different colors because there were just the two bridesmaids in the wedding party. I have always thought their dresses to be unique.
LOIS DOBRADENKA
SHELBY TOWNSHIP, MI

I see us outside St. Mary's on that October day in 1982. Rich pops the champagne as everyone cheers our newly wedded life.

DARLENE BUECHEL · CHILTON, WI

SHARED ANNIVERSARIES

The first of October is a special date for descendants of Dewey and Ruth Bunner, who were married on that day in 1916. Since then, five couples in their extended family have married on Oct. 1, including the three pictured here. Harriet Bunner, Dewey and Ruth's daughter, married Herbert Dady in 1937 (lower right); Barbara Bunner, Harriet's sister, married John Shinn in 1949 (left); and Timothy Dady, Harriet's son, married Maureen Kay Moran in 1968. The most recent Oct. 1 weddings in our family were Tim Dady Jr.'s marriage to Hope Howard in 1998 and Annette Leschewski's to Douglas Taylor in 1999. Annette, my daughter, is the granddaughter of Harriet and Herbert.

JUDY DADY LESCHEWSKI · DECATUR, IL

Sidney scooped up Shelly in his arms and carried her home.

Friendly in Flatbush

His pickup line proved quite literal.

During my last year of junior high school, in 1958, we moved to a neighborhood in East Flatbush/ Brownsville, Brooklyn, New York. It was rough at first, but I finally made friends with a girl named Sarah and often visited her after school.

After I made a few trips to her family's apartment, Sarah asked me if I'd like to meet her friend Sidney, who lived in the building next door. I agreed, not thinking too much about it. A few days later I was at her home when she looked out her kitchen window and said, "He's here."

"Who?" I asked.

"Sidney," she said. "Let's go!"

There he was, standing outside her window. *What a macho guy,* I thought. His dark, wavy hair curled down the center of his forehead, similar to the style Fonzie wore on the TV show *Happy Days,* only this was well before that time.

I swooned and tried not to show it as Sidney and I made casual conversation about his exploits the day before in the schoolyard where, according to him, "the guys tossed around a girl they knew like a football."

"What do you mean?" I asked, rather naively.

I don't remember whether I was just startled or totally impressed.

"Like this," he said, and he lifted me up. "We're going home," he added. I asked Sarah if it would be all right with her if we left. I suspected that she also had a crush on Sidney.

"It's OK," she told us.

My home was a few blocks away, and he carried me as if I was a featherweight. Once there, we sat and talked on the bench outside. My mom saw him from a distance when she returned home and told me later that she thought I was talking to a teacher. He looked much more mature than I did.

When he told me he was 17 and asked my age, something told me not to say 14½. So I said I was 15.

The next day he told Sarah he wanted to call me and "drag me to the beach." So, she gave him my number.

We looked at romance differently then, that's for sure. But this was the real thing. Sidney and I were married in 1965. After being married to my macho guy for more than 50 years —and three children later—I can truly say he's been the best husband that any gal could possibly have.

SHELLY SITZER · CHARLOTTESVILLE, VA

A Night to Remember

Three things I remember from prom on May 14, 1944: my date's name, Gordon May; where it took place, Hotel Argonne in Lima, Ohio; and what I wore, a pink satin formal with a borrowed fur jacket. After 74 years, how can anyone expect me to remember all the things that took place back then?

LEE WILLIAMS · LIMA, OH

CHAPTER 4

....

RETRO FUN

Relive the pleasures of days gone by when
a game of Scrabble or racing in a Soap
Box Derby brought out our best.

Daily Dipping

Summers in the city were spent at the community pool, where kids young
and old soaked up the warm sunshine and splashed in the cool water
for hours. My Uncle Merle took this photo on a hot day.

CHUCK BELLING · MADISON, WI

Performers at Weeki Wachee Springs in Spring Hill, Florida, hold air hoses that allow them to breathe and remain submerged for programs lasting up to 45 minutes. Visitors filled the 400-seat auditorium to watch the underwater ballet.

A Dream Ripples Through Time

One showman's innovation left a deep impression.

Central Florida in the 1950s and '60s had many roadside attractions, including Marineland, Silver Springs and Cypress Gardens, but my favorite was Weeki Wachee, a theme park built around a freshwater spring in Hernando County.

Seated in the auditorium, with its large picture windows that looked into the depths 16 feet below the surface, I was mesmerized by women dressed as mermaids performing underwater ballets. While submerged, the mermaids could eat a banana and drink from a soda bottle.

For weeks after our visits, I'd practice the mermaids' moves in our pool at home. I even learned to eat and drink underwater, too.

I didn't have to go far for help mastering the tricks. My father was Newton A. "Newt" Perry, who founded Weeki Wachee in 1947.

Newt was an innovator and performer. He got into show business in the 1920s doing short documentaries with Grantland Rice, a popular sportswriter whose Sportlight Film shorts would run in movie theaters before the feature.

Newt went on to be technical adviser on the *Tarzan* movies and a stunt double for actor Johnny Weissmuller in the 1930s. And in World War II, he trained frogmen, members of the Navy unit that grew into the SEAL program.

But my father's dream was to build an underwater attraction. When he opened Weeki Wachee, he did the shows there with a few local women he recruited to be mermaids. He taught them to breathe using air hoses hidden around the underwater sets, a technique that allowed them to remain submerged for up to 45 minutes and which is still used at the park.

It's remarkable that Newt's dream continues more than 70 years later. Now a state park, Weeki Wachee still has the power to mesmerize anyone lucky enough to visit there.

DELEE PERRY · OCALA, FL

THE PAST SPRINGS ETERNAL: WEEKI WACHEE THEN & NOW

The Seminole name Weeki Wachee means "little spring" or "winding river."

....

The spring is believed to be the deepest in the U.S. Its caverns have been explored to a depth of 407 feet, but the bottom hasn't been found.

....

The spring pumps about 117 million gallons a day of fresh, 74-degree water into the Weeki Wachee River, which wends 12 miles to the Gulf of Mexico.

....

Submerged signs warn divers away from its most treacherous caves. Certain areas can be explored only during droughts, when the current slows down.

....

When Newt Perry scouted the area for his roadside park in the '40s, the spring was clogged with appliances, old cars and other junk.

....

Perry built his auditorium into the spring's limestone shelf. It forms a natural theater on a slope 16 to 20 feet below the surface, where the current is a robust 5 mph. Mermaids work hard to stay in place.

....

The first show was Oct. 13, 1947. Mermaids weren't paid, but they did get free meals and bathing suits.

....

In 1959, steady promotion by new owner ABC kicked off the park's most successful period.

....

It joined Florida's state park system in 2008 and has a $13 adult gate fee. Mermaids perform three times daily.

Newt Perry before and after Weeki Wachee: setting up a unique picnic for a 1942 short film (top); and with daughter Delee and wife Dorothy in 1970.

Electric boat tours of the canals at Cypress Gardens provided intimate views of tropical flora. The tours started in 1937 and remained popular throughout the park's history.

Where Wishes Were Free

A day at Cypress Gardens offered a peaceful retreat from war.

Located in former swampland along the shore of Lake Eloise in Winter Haven, Florida, Cypress Gardens as seen through my 5-year-old eyes in 1944 was very different from the national tourist attraction it later became.

We lived in Auburndale, about 6 miles from the park. The war years were tough: Gas and automobile tires were rationed and scarce, money for family outings even scarcer.

Fortunately, Dick and Julie Pope, the owners of Cypress Gardens, held a Polk County Day once a year, when local residents could get into the beautiful park for free.

For the whole day we forgot our hardships and strolled paths through a fairyland of bougainvilleas, gardenias, azaleas and roses. My favorite was the one I called the bashful plant, though it was probably a touch-me-not (*Mimosa pudica*). The leaves would shrink and close up when I touched them, much as I, a shy girl, felt like doing around people.

I looked forward to seeing the banyan tree, which was planted the year I was born, 1939, and has grown to giant proportions today.

And I stopped at the Wishing Tree, a huge oak damaged in a hurricane, a large limb almost completely torn away. Though partially detached from the mother tree, the limb thrived. A nearby sign promised that if you sat on it and made a wish, your wish would come true. Every year I asked for the same thing—to fly like the birds inhabiting the pines and cypresses in the gardens. My three brothers teased me that it couldn't come true, but the first time I got on a plane, I knew the Wishing Tree had proved them wrong.

CG.17—"Cypress Gardens Aqua Maids"

Cypress Trees and Knees In Florida Cypress Gardens

Daring shows on Lake Eloise made Cypress Gardens the "water-skiing capital of the world."

2023 AQUAPLANING AT THE FLORIDA CYPRESS GARDENS

FROM SWAMP TO SWANK: CYPRESS GARDENS' RISE

IN 1931, DICK AND JULIE POPE BOUGHT several acres of cypress swamp on Lake Eloise in Winter Haven, Florida, for a tourist garden. It took five years to clear the land, dig canals and procure the plants. Cypress Gardens opened Jan. 2, 1936; 182 visitors each paid 25 cents to get in.

The gardens featured more than 30 kinds of palms, 26 varieties of banana trees, 40 varieties of azalea and 30 kinds of camellias. Plants came from Africa, Asia, Oceania and the Americas.

When frost killed vines at the garden gates in 1940, Julie had a staff member in a hooped dress stand nearby to divert visitors' attention. Roaming southern belles were soon added as regular fixtures.

In 1941, when a newspaper printed a picture of the gardens with water-skiers, several servicemen showed up to see the skiing show. There was no such thing at the time, but on the spot, Julie rounded up her kids and friends to put one on. Cypress Gardens has been credited with making water-skiing a craze that lasted well into the 1970s.

A tireless promoter, Dick was known to say to his staff, "I've called the press and told them something big is happening here today. Any ideas?"

The Pope family sold the park in 1985. After several owners, closings and reopenings, the gardens became part of Legoland Florida in 2010, and joined the National Register of Historic Places in 2014.

For 25 cents, visitors could tour the canals in small boats. These rides weren't in our budget, but we enjoyed standing on the wooden bridges as the boats passed below us. I admired the southern belles who roamed the gardens in colorful hooped dresses. At lunch, we'd picnic in the shade.

Between water-ski shows, guests could swim in the lake. There was even a rope tied to one of the cypresses at the shore. What a thrill to swing out and drop in the water. This activity ended when more ski shows were added.

We visited Cypress Gardens on Polk County Day every year until the Popes discontinued the event in the early 1950s. What memories!

BEVERLY SCOTT · AUBURNDALE, FL

The seedling banyan tree planted in 1939 is massive today.

Dan and Karen cut a rug to the Average White Band's "Cut the Cake."

Bumped into the Big Time

It was their chance to get down with disco.

W e had just started dating in 1975 in Kettering, Ohio, when I asked my gal, Karen, if she wanted to take ballroom dancing lessons. She agreed, and it didn't take long before everyone, the instructors in particular, realized Karen was a Dancer with a capital D.

As a teenager she'd danced with a troupe and did solos at fairs around the state. She'd won the talent portions of beauty pageants with her dancing, and choreographed shows across Ohio.

Our studio was participating in a local dance exhibition, which was to feature national ballroom dancing champions and other top-ranked hoofers. One of the instructors approached us about demonstrating the latest disco craze: the bump.

Karen worked me hard for that two-minute routine. Many long hours and aching muscles later, she finally showed me some mercy.

"Well," she said, "I guess that's as good as this is going to get."

Karen and I arrived at the exhibition, which was held at a school gym, to find out that we were to perform first. The funky sounds of the Average White Band's "Cut the Cake" filled the hall, and we bumped and hustled our way through our well-practiced routine. Someone even captured the whole thing on film. The studio paid us a grand sum of $20, which I later joked made us official dancing professionals.

After the show, the visiting dancers and studio instructors had a private party, and to my surprise they invited us. I soon figured out why: All of the pros—the real pros—were itching to dance with Karen. She spent the rest of the night doing tangos, rumbas and waltzes with those guys.

At one point I reminded her to "save the last dance for me."

She did. We've been married for more than 40 years.

DAN GRAHAM · GREENVILLE, SC

STAYIN' ALIVE AT THE RINK

SEVERAL FRIENDS AND I DECIDED to go roller-skating one night in the mid-1970s. Even though I had never done it, I thought I'd be able to skate, considering that I'd mastered riding a unicycle. Once on the rink, though, I realized quickly that sitting and controlling one wheel was a breeze compared to trying to corral four wheels on each foot. I was courting disaster and I knew it.

Did I mention that this was during the height of the disco era? The place was exactly as you might imagine it—a huge mirror ball hanging at center ceiling, everyone in gaudy polyester, and the Bee Gees pumping through the stereo system at earthquake-level decibels.

For the first hour, I was on my backside more than I was standing (let alone skating). So it wasn't only my pride that was hurting. To top it off, there was a guy gliding around who thought he was God's gift to Donna Summer. Not only could he skate forward *and* backward, he was able to do so to the rhythm of each song. I wasn't jealous of his skills, but I was annoyed that he would point at me and chuckle every time I fell.

By the last song, this rolling John Travolta was doing the wheeled version of "The Hustle" all over the rink. His favorite trick was to twirl in complete circles while smiling at me.

Just as he passed me in what I hoped was the final assault on my battered self-worth, he suddenly lost his balance. And, you guessed it, Mr. Disco landed flat on *his* backside. I saw my chance and took it. I pointed at the guy, laughed and yelled, "Thank you, Lord!"

I never attempted to skate again, but I will always have fond memories of how that night ended.

ROB MEYERS · GILBERT, AZ

BOOGIE NIGHTS
As teenagers, Danny, Michael, Kathy and Colleen would go disco dancing on Saturday nights in the early 1980s in Willoughby, Ohio. They kept asking us to go with them, but we were reluctant—imagine 40-plus parents disco dancing with their kids! One night we finally gave in and we had a wonderful time. I still like disco music and dancing to this day.
CAROLYN NAGY
AIKEN, SC

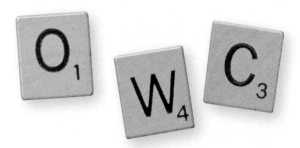

EPIC BATTLES TURNED 'MURRIENT'

WHEN ONE OF US SHOUTED "LET'S PLAY A GAME!" that usually meant Scrabble. Although one corner of the burgundy box was held together with yellowed and peeling tape, it was still our favorite. Our version had only one true blank tile, as we had etched an A on one and an L on another in ballpoint pen.

A 14-year span separated the oldest sibling from the youngest in our family. Any time we played, there was much cheating, usually in favor of the youngest. "Let me see your letters," we'd say, and then we'd all brainstorm on how to get the most points.

We kept our two-letter word list handy, and many of our X, Y and Z words came from it, including *ex, ax* and *xi.* For the Z, if we couldn't find two O's together, we'd look for an A to spell *za.*

Our best games were late at night, when exhaustion made us silly. Nonsense words and challenges flew around the table. One night, my middle brother coined the word *murrient.* And the argument began.

"That's not a word!"

"Is too!"

"Well, it's not English!"

"Is too!"

"Use it in a sentence!"

"That's not murrient."

We let it stand, though *murrient,* which turned out to be Latin meaning "squeak like mice," became a family byword after that. We would use it in a variety of ways and always with laughter.

One Scrabble game played in the dead of winter has gone down in family history. My cousin Suzy was visiting and got pulled into a game that included my father. Midway through, Dad grew tired of it—he wasn't winning—so the board "accidentally" flew up from the table and landed on the floor. Suzy still laughs about it.

Our old version of Scrabble is gone. The new one is huge and spins on a turntable. But sadly, it gathers dust as we play lengthy spells of the game Words with Friends on our smartphones and computers.

At least we can't end our competitions by throwing the game board anymore.

SANDRA BREWSTER
GLENVILLE, NY

MOM'S THE WORD: SHE'S UNBEATABLE

Mom and Dad—Dorothy and Joseph—played Scrabble almost every night. Neither gave the other any special consideration. Mom was always out to win.

A few years after Dad died, Mom moved into a senior residence, where she found three men in her building who would join her once a week for a game of Scrabble. She still won most of the time, but the guys enjoyed her company and the challenge.

KATHY COREY · ST. LOUIS, MO

SCRABBLE SCRIBBLES

Architect Alfred Mosher Butts invented an early version of the game in 1933.

·················

It was originally called Lexiko, a short form variation of *lexicon,* meaning "vocabulary" or "language."

·················

Initially, no game manufacturers were interested in it. Butts and his business partner, James Brunot, an entrepreneur and game lover, began producing the game themselves and called it Scrabble, which means "to grope frantically."

·················

About 33 percent of American homes own a Scrabble game.

·················

Competitors in the North American Scrabble Players Association's annual championship tournament use tiles that are smooth on both sides so they can't tell the blanks from the lettered tiles when selecting them from the bag.

Scrabble comes in 29 languages. More than 150 million games have been sold worldwide.

Box suppers often included sweets such as cookies or pies. In this busy kitchen, Madeline Atwater rolls pie dough to a perfect crust as Beverly Zimmerman notes the proper technique to use.

Box Supper Bombshell

By auction time, everyone knew the secret of the colored ribbons.

Box supper weather occurs in the late fall before winter starts. Usually by this time of year there has already been a killing frost, so the trees are enriched by beautiful colors. The watermelons and gardens are long gone, and pumpkins can be seen among the turnip patches, not yet harvested. Soon the persimmons will start ripening.

During this special time of year, most schools in the county where I grew up would have a box supper. This was a favorite means of raising money. The young ladies of the school district decorated boxes and filled them with homemade cookies, pies, sandwiches and even full meals. Inside each box, the woman would include a piece of paper with her name. At a specified time they would secretly deliver the boxes to the school so no one would guess whose box belonged to whom.

The boxes were auctioned to raise money. Naturally, each married man knew which was his wife's and was expected to bid on it. The real competition was among unmarried men, who would bid on the most attractive box and share the contents with the young lady who had brought it. Sometimes, real dates would ensue.

One of my teachers, Anne, had a boyfriend, Fred. The day of the box supper, my friends Bill and John overheard a conversation between the couple. Anne told Fred that her box would have a red, white and blue ribbon on top of the white handle. He couldn't miss it.

Bill and John immediately spread the news to the other young men in town who were interested in bidding for Miss Anne's box supper. But they didn't stop there. They also persuaded several young ladies to decorate their boxes the same way. Now the stage was set.

Bidding at the box supper that night was frantic. Six similarly decorated boxes were auctioned off, and Fred was outbid on all but the last one. When the final box with the pretty patriotic ribbon came up, Fred bid 25 cents and won, because everyone else had spent their money on the counterfeit boxes. He was lucky enough to get the one made by Miss Anne. Bill and John, watching from the sidelines, laughed hysterically.

For the first time, a teacher's box sold for the low bid. Even so, the evening raised more money than anyone could remember. It was a success, and everyone found their box supper cooks and enjoyed the evening.

Box suppers were a highlight in our rural community. They were an inexpensive kind of entertainment that gave us a reason to get together, taking our minds off the problems of making a living.

NEAL MURPHY · SAN AUGUSTINE, TX

VINTAGE ADS · VINTAGE ADS

BUSIEST ROOM IN THE HOUSE

Bathrooms have received some colorful attention over the years. Do you remember these items?

1972 »

Cloud Variations

This eye-catching Sears ad ran a full page in *Better Homes and Gardens*. It describes a dizzying number of possible combinations—ovals, oblongs, rounds and contours, with or without fringe, and in 13 colors. Who knew choosing a humble bath rug could be so complicated?

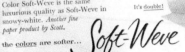

« 1956

Pretty in Pastel

Soft-Weve was among the first to make toilet paper in the pinks, blues, greens and yellows of midcentury bathrooms—because who wouldn't want to match the paper to the fixtures? Colored toilet paper was popular into the 1970s, when sales waned amid warnings that it could cause skin irritation and that the dyes were damaging the environment.

Marching to the Same Beat

Music strikes a major chord for everyone in the family.

——

My family's symphony of life started before I was born. When my dad, Edward Kulesza, was in high school, he loved to listen to his neighbor, a professional saxophone player, practicing his music. Dad was so mesmerized by it that he decided to try to play sax in his school band. Unfortunately, the only horn available was a trombone. Dad gave it his best, but he had to quit at 16 when he left school to get a job to help support his family.

Flash forward a few decades to when I played alto saxophone at Royal Oak Dondero High School at the urging of—you guessed it—my dad. He strongly encouraged me to follow a musical path and was wonderful about my practice sessions, even though he needed to rest in the evenings before he went to his second job. If Mom would start to chastise me, Dad would say, "No, I want to hear her play as I go to sleep."

Dondero High used to host a yearly cavalcade of area high school marching bands. At one of these events my friends and I were walking by the field stands when we noticed a large group of people huddled near something on the ground. It seemed that someone had dropped a trumpet, and the horn was down for the count. We all had a good laugh about the idiot who'd fumbled his instrument.

Well, it gets even funnier: I married that idiot. Brian and I met in college, and it was only when we were dating seriously that I found out he was the poor guy who'd dropped his trumpet at the high school band event. (His parents later had the horn repaired.)

Brian and I discovered another surprising connection. Remember the saxophone-playing neighbor who had inspired my father, who in turn encouraged me to pursue music? That was George Lupanoff, my husband's grandfather.

Now our song plays on through our daughter Kim Pullen, a percussionist with a degree in music performance. She went to Brian's high school. At a special reunion event, all three of us marched and played with the band on the football field. It was a dream come true for this old band geek.

CHERYL KULESZA BURNEY
ROYAL OAK, MI

Clockwise from top left: Cheryl and her alto sax in her sophomore year, 1979-'80; Cheryl's dad, Edward, who passed on his love of music; Brian and his ill-fated trumpet, years before its downfall; the Burneys' daughter Kim, who earned a bachelor's degree in music performance.

TOE TAPPING

SKIRTING AROUND THE ISSUE

When I started cello in the fifth grade in 1962, girls had to wear only skirts or dresses to school. But I had special permission to wear pants on the days that I had lessons or orchestra practice.
GENEVE HARRIS · ROCKFORD, IL

MOTHER-DAUGHTER DUET

At age 10 in 1958, I started taking lessons on a 12-button bass accordion in our small city of Fremont, Nebraska. My mother basically learned along with me and we both became quite good. We'd play during Saturday night get-togethers. The adults tipped their whiskey highballs and glasses of beer while tapping their feet to our rendition of "Beer Barrel Polka."
ANAMARIE WOSTRCHILL · CENTENNIAL, CO

TWO CAN PLAY THAT TUNE

My dad was a big fan of accordionist Myron Floren on *The Lawrence Welk Show*. Before I knew it, he'd signed up my sister and me for lessons, and within a year, we were performing as a duet at business luncheons, club meetings and retirement homes. In this picture from 1955, I'm 8 (left) and Karen is 6.
KRISTINE ANN SHELL · REDLANDS, CA

PREACHING TO THE CHOIR

My daddy was a preacher and told my music teachers that he wanted me to learn "so one day she can play for church." I took piano in Texas until we moved to Virginia, where he bought me a red accordion and I began lessons. More than 65 years later I still have that accordion and still play it. It has my name on it, though somehow they managed to misspell it as "Sissie."

MARY "SISSY" SOMMERS STOVALL
CLEVELAND, TN

DRESS REHEARSAL

This is my father-in-law, John Ashton, in 1918, at age 8, all spruced up for his violin recital. We enjoyed his playing for years at family gatherings.

PHILIP ELDER · WEST PALM BEACH, FL

PICK OF THE PACK

Dad signed me up for a steel-guitar class in Joplin, Missouri, in 1949, when I was 9. As a top student, I was featured on a Sunday radio promotion. In high school in Memphis, Tennessee, I played in a country band with classmate Larry "Red" Manuel, who was later inducted into the Rockabilly Hall of Fame.

ROLAND SNEED
BLUE SPRINGS, MO

ON YOUR MARK, GET SET, GO!

NO ENGINE NEEDED
The Scouts sponsored the 1946 Soap Box Derby in Susanville, California. Boys prep to race down Main Street.
PHOTO COURTESY OF LASSEN HISTORICAL SOCIETY · SUSANVILLE, CA

DAD-MADE MOTOR CAR
My husband, William, couldn't throw anything away. In 1959, using a motor and wheels from a discarded lawn mower, he built a go-kart for our kids, Bill and Shirley. They drove the motor car around the supermarket parking lot.
MARTHA MAHON · TRENTON, NJ

ONE PUSH REQUIRED
We called it a pushie, and in 1954 my brother Dennis, standing, and I raced it down the hilly streets of our Pottstown, Pennsylvania, neighborhood. Ours was always the fastest. My grandfather was caretaker for a local estate, and the owner gave him a set of professional-looking Soap Box Derby wheels with ball bearings and iron axles. We rigged a steering wheel to a rope to control the front tires.
ALAN KLINE · POTTSTOWN, PA

COURTING FAVORS

Getting ready for the Soap Box Derby in Coshocton, Ohio, when I was 12, gave me the butterflies. My dad and I used old crates from my uncle's appliance store to build the car. I won the first heat but lost the second. My youngest daughter and her husband now display the car in their pole barn.
RICHARD STAFFORD
FRAZEYSBURG, OH

ALL-AROUND HANDYMAN

My father could fix, build and drive anything. He built his first car at 15. Next he built a dragster, then dune buggies. To me he was Superman. I was one lucky girl to have David Hutchinson as my dad!
SUSAN HUTCHINSON
SAN DIMAS, CA

WINTER GAMES

SLEDDING SQUAD

Our dad, Frank Lyons, would load our station wagon with sleds and kids and off we'd go. Here we are at Bradys Run Park in Beaver Falls, Pennsylvania, in January 1966: my sister Susan, my brother Paul, neighbors Pete and David Matich, me and my brother Tim.

JUDY THARP · MONACA, PA

D-I-Y SLED

Willamette Valley in Oregon has a mild climate with little snow. But on this winter day in 1982, Mother Nature dropped over 6 inches in our area. Bob, my husband, tied a rope to a Hunt's box and pulled our 2-year-old son Cooper up and down the street. Then they came home for some hot cocoa.

ROBBIE WRIGHT
EUGENE, OR

My uncle Merle was an avid skier and an amateur photographer. I found this picture of skiers dressed as snow bunnies in his collection of slides, which record more than 20 years of his skiing travels.

CHUCK BELLING · MADISON, WI

CHAPTER 5

AT
WORK

Read touching accounts of hard work
and tenacity, the kind that gets us all
through tough times.

Folded Pairs

During the first half of the 20th century, the Phoenix Hosiery Co. was a mainstay in downtown Milwaukee, Wisconsin. Working in one of the company's six plants, these factory workers folded and packed the product for seamless shipping nationwide.

The Phoenix Hosiery Co. owned several buildings in Milwaukee's Third Ward district.

Stocking Stuffers

A once-thriving hosiery factory met a fickle fate.

Soon after moving from Beloit, Wisconsin, to Milwaukee in 1968, my career path took a couple of interesting turns. I was intrigued by airplanes and started working in the data processing and reservation departments for North Central Airlines. But when the company consolidated functions in its Minneapolis headquarters, I decided to stay in Milwaukee and look for something else.

I eventually found work in the distribution center at Kayser-Roth Corp., housed in the Phoenix Building near the heart of downtown Milwaukee. Kayser-Roth had purchased the Phoenix Hosiery Co., and by the late 1960s, all production had moved to North Carolina. What remained in Milwaukee

PHOENIX HOSIERY CO.

Based in Milwaukee, Wisconsin, from 1897 to 1959

....

Barbara Newberry, a performer with the Ziegfeld Follies, modeled Phoenix hosiery in a 1929 ad campaign

....

Sold to Kayser-Roth Corp. in 1959

....

Production moved to North Carolina, but warehousing and shipping remained in Milwaukee until 1973

were the warehouse and shipping functions. I ran the warehouse and managed the office personnel; I'm a people person, so it was a great fit.

But fashions changed and so did the hosiery business. As women began to wear more pantsuits and slacks, stockings and pantyhose went out of style.

I worked there until the mid-'70s, when the company decided to close the office and move all remaining functions to North Carolina.

While clearing everything out, I discovered a discarded box that was filled with newsletters and these company photos from the 1930s and '40s. It was fun to look back at the early, flourishing days of this business.

GARY JENSEN
OCONOMOWOC, WI

WORKERS TAKE PRIDE IN FANCY FOOTWORK

1. High standards at the Phoenix Hosiery plant required eight major inspections. **2.** Winding thread from spools to cones was called coning and made the knitting process smoother. **3.** Menders worked with their hands instead of machines. **4.** Stockings, shaped on boards after dyeing, moved along an assembly line into dryers.

Sisters Bring the Heat

One specific skill set gave them
steady work during WWII.

At a family reunion in 2016, my cousin's wife insisted that I tell the story of my mom and her two sisters. I had the photos, along with other documents my mom had saved in a scrapbook. One photo shows my mom, Elaine Carlson, and her sisters Ruth and June wearing welding masks, jackets and gloves during World War II. The trio moved from Minnesota to Indiana in 1941 and worked as welders until the war ended in 1945.

Here's how they landed in Indiana.

My mom's dad, Gustaf, was a Swedish immigrant who became a tenant farmer in northwest Minnesota. He married Clara and the couple settled in Red Lake, where they raised eight children— four boys and four girls.

My mom was born in 1921 and graduated from Kelliher High School in 1939. Afterward she went to work in the hospital kitchen in Duluth where her older sister Ruth was studying to be a nurse. There she met my dad, Lester Pelander, while he was recuperating from a skiing accident.

Three sisters—from left, June, Elaine and Ruth Carlson—shared a room for $8 a month.

When war was declared on Dec. 8, 1941, everything changed. Dad, who had been a Duluth-area skier, joined the military and was sent to the Aleutian Islands as a ski instructor. My mom and Ruth were joined by their youngest sister, June, who had graduated by that time. The three women attended Zenith vocational training school to learn welding. Once they finished, they were approached by a recruiter, Joe Morris, from Jeffersonville Boat & Machine Co. in Jeffersonville, Indiana. He interviewed them at noon, and that night they were on a train to Indiana.

My mom and my aunts were among the many women who went to work in factories to support the war effort. All three worked in a factory welding LSTs (an acronym for Landing Ship, Tank), which were used to transport troops, vehicles and supplies during missions to France, Sicily and Italy, and in the Pacific. They roomed together at a boarding house in New Albany, Indiana. When the war ended in 1945, all three returned to Minnesota to rekindle relationships and start new lives.

ROD PELANDER
FERGUSON, MO

When war was declared on Dec. 8, 1941, everything changed.

Learning the ropes, youngest sister June kneels while Ruth, left, and Elaine give her pointers.

First Impressions Count

Your past is a good indication of what you'll do in the future.

G etting my first official job when I turned 16 in 1959 taught me valuable skills. John Monsour, a pleasant, hardworking man and the owner of Penhurst Fruit Market, wanted me to work for him. My mother and grandmother were longtime shoppers and he admired their reputations.

He hired me to work after school and all day on Saturdays. My starting wage was 30 cents an hour, but Mr. Monsour told me that once I learned the job and became more valuable, he would increase my pay to 85 cents an hour, close to minimum wage.

When I started, I needed to overcome my shyness. I learned to greet customers, establish a rapport with them, and earn their trust so that they would return. My duties expanded, and soon I was waiting on customers, displaying and watering the produce, washing windows, raking sawdust from the floors, and delivering groceries.

I worked hard and it paid off. The job kept me away from the neighborhood mischief. And at the beginning of my senior year in high school, Mr. Monsour raised my wage to $1 an hour. He told me not to tell the other workers. Mum was the word; I wasn't going to mess up my good thing!

My earnings enabled me to buy school clothes, and I no longer had to think about

Harry's wages allowed him to dress well while attending Westinghouse High School in Pittsburgh in 1961.

dropping out because I didn't have the right things to wear. I became more confident, gregarious and self-sufficient. I paid my way and felt useful and important to my family.

After high school, I worked through college and earned an MBA in finance. I was offered a dream job in Washington, D.C., doing international banking, a position requiring a security clearance. I got the job.

Later, while visiting my family in Pittsburgh, I stopped at the fruit market to say hello to Mr. Monsour. He joked that I had brought the feds down on him.

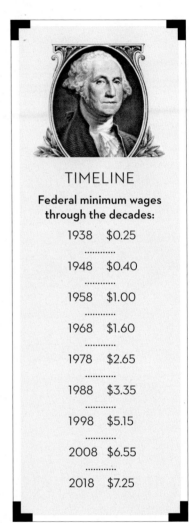

TIMELINE

Federal minimum wages through the decades:

1938	$0.25
1948	$0.40
1958	$1.00
1968	$1.60
1978	$2.65
1988	$3.35
1998	$5.15
2008	$6.55
2018	$7.25

I thought: *Wow, they went to my high school employer to ask about me and my work performance.*

My mother always told me: "Harry, every job you do is important, so always do your best." I learned early the wisdom of those words.

HARRY JAMES FORD
PITTSBURGH, PA

Rosario (far left) and brothers Giuseppe and Andrea staff the barbershop they built in Gary, Indiana.

With Only $2 in His Pocket

He built a life doing what he knew best.

My husband, Rosario Cammarata, arrived in the United States from Sicily in 1958 with his mother, two brothers and $2 his father had given him. The family settled in Gary, Indiana, but Rosario was forced to quit high school and find a job to support his mother and siblings. He was considered a master barber back in Sicily, so he got a job at a barbershop.

After two years, his boss asked if he wanted to buy the shop. Because Rosario had saved his money, he was able to buy his first barbershop in downtown Gary at 18.

In 1966, he built a barbershop and an adjoining building in a Gary neighborhood with help from his brothers. We got married that year and went to Italy for two months. When we returned, Rosario started Gary's first soccer league for adults.

By 1977, we had three sons and moved to Lake Havasu City, Arizona, where Rosario opened a one-man shop in a mall. He worked for almost 10 years there. Once again, Rosario's love of soccer prompted him to start the city's first soccer league.

The family moved to Phoenix in 1987 and Rosario worked for Smitty's Barbershop for a short while before buying his own shop in Mesa. After a few years his brothers joined him again and eventually he bought another shop in Scottsdale. Rosario ran one shop and one of his brothers ran the other. By April 2016, the brothers had sold both shops.

Rosario now has dementia and no longer runs a barbershop, but he can still cut hair. He often gets together with former employees to trade stories about the old shop and the great times they had.

So at 16, Rosario came to America with only $2 in his pocket, yet went on to make an amazing life for himself and his entire family.

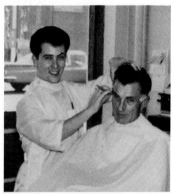

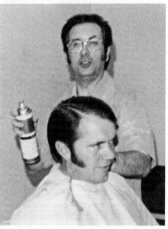

Rosario cuts hair in his shops in downtown Gary, Indiana (top), and in Lake Havasu City, Arizona.

CAROL CAMMARATA
CAVE CREEK, AZ

Service Came with a Smile

Her positive attitude earned praise.

Times were tough in the 1930s. After my mother, Bertha May Royston Crossley, lost her dad when she was 11, staying in school became a luxury. So she quit school when she was old enough and went to work. She was hired at a local sewing factory in Shrewsbury, Pennsylvania, despite having only an eighth-grade education.

While at the factory, she met my dad, Thomas Crossley, and they were soon married. Afterward, she stayed home with her three children until the youngest, me, was in the third grade. Then she decided it was time she went out and got a job.

Lacking education and experience, she was hired by Sears, Roebuck and Co. for an entry-level job in the garden shop. But when an office job opened, she applied and was put in charge of the routing desk.

School let out earlier than Mom got off work, so on many days I would meet her at Sears. I had a grand time waiting at her office. On occasion, Mom would hand me a ticket to file in the cubby next to her desk. I felt so important, so sure that I was helping her. Then she would give me a quarter and I would buy a hot dog from the deli downstairs.

A big part of her job was talking to customers on the phone and letting them know when their purchases would be delivered. Sometimes the customers became impatient because deliveries were late or something arrived damaged. But no matter the mood of the customer, Mom always spoke quietly and calmed many potential storms for Sears.

At the end of each day, she walked around the store to pick up order tickets, and took them back to her desk to schedule the deliveries.

I was so proud of my mom. She dressed professionally and always wore a smile. Everyone had friendly words for her as she passed their stations. And she took every chance to greet her fellow workers as she walked past.

Those were good times, and I have warm memories of spending so many afternoons with my mom. I acquired my good work ethic from watching and following her example.

E.M. "COOKIE" MILLER
YELM, WA

SEARS TIMELINE

1886
Richard W. Sears launches a mail-order business selling watches.

1887
Alvah C. Roebuck joins Sears as a watch repairer.

1893
The partners officially call their company Sears, Roebuck and Co.

1924
Sears launches a Chicago, Illinois, radio station, eventually settling on call letters WLS (World's Largest Store).

1925
The first retail Sears store opens in Chicago.

1933
Sears issues its first Christmas Book, renamed the Wish Book in 1968.

2005
Major merger. Sears and Kmart.

Five years before she retired at Sears, Bertha got written up on the board— big kudos from her boss.

This Goede family photo was taken in 1960 at Mader's restaurant in Milwaukee, Wisconsin. From left: Julie, Sandy, Olivia, Paul, Diane and Steve.

Teach a Man to Cook

While others ate his food, Dad dreamed up new dishes.

B oth of my parents worked in the 1950s while my siblings and I were growing up in our small town in southern Wisconsin. My mother, Olivia Goede, was a registered nurse at Edgerton Hospital, and my father, Paul, was a chef. In the early 1960s, he worked at Mader's, a top German restaurant in Milwaukee, Wisconsin.

Like most chefs, he was always experimenting with different food combinations and new recipes. He finished third in 1960 in a national sandwich contest with his creation "Dreamy, Creamy, Nutty Tuna." My sister Sandy came up with the name.

His winnings included a trip to New York City. After airfare and the tailored suit my father purchased for the trip, my mother guessed he barely broke even. Regardless, the whole family was proud of Dad and the work he did.

The tuna sandwich was not his only prizewinning recipe. He won a dessert contest sponsored by the Door County (Wisconsin) Cherry Association, and that earned the family a week's stay at the Anderson Hotel in Ephraim in Door County.

Then in the 1980s, when he was food service director for the University of Wisconsin-Stout, Dad won a contest sponsored by the Citrus Growers of Florida for his recipe for *boeuf en croute* with orange sauce.

My father often did catering jobs that included the whole family, and my mom worked full time and raised four kids. We were so lucky to have parents who encouraged creativity and instilled a strong work ethic in all of us.

DIANE GOEDE LUTZ
BEAVER DAM, WI

Farm Futures

Rural life replaced city style.

Seventy-six years ago, I was in my early 20s and I was ready to conquer the working world.

I lived at Lorraine Apartments in Spencer, Iowa, near the old library. My roommate, Leone Shaeffer, and I were literal roommates: Instead of an apartment, we shared the apartment owner's bedroom on the first floor, while the owner slept on a cot in her living room. We also shared her bathroom. Breakfast was included in our modest rent. Our landlady didn't charge much, which was good because we didn't get paid a lot.

Weekdays, I walked several blocks daily to the Clay County Courthouse, where I worked as a deputy auditor. After work, I would meet Leone, who worked at the American Automobile Association office. We often stopped by The Woman Shop on the east side of Main Street as we walked home.

We couldn't afford the latest stylish clothes, but we loved to browse. Even though we didn't wear hats, we liked to try them on. And when we had money, we'd buy a new dress for work.

This was during World War II, when women's nylon stockings were scarce and expensive. If we didn't have nylons, we went barelegged. Sometimes a clerk at The Woman Shop would save a light beige pair of stockings with a seam up the back behind the counter for us.

The shop owner, Mr. Dvergsten (known as Mr. D),

Stella worked as a deputy auditor but left to marry. She kept the books on the family farm for more than 70 years.

often rang up the sales himself. We didn't have credit cards, so Mr. D would write up a sales slip with a carbon copy and stamp it "ON APPROVAL" in big letters. No money changed hands. In a day or two, I would either return the item or pay him.

My job at the courthouse was a good position in the early 1940s, but I left when I got married. Looking back, my husband, Donald, and I could have used the extra money. But things were different then,

and I happily became one of the many stay-at-home wives of my generation.

My friends at the courthouse sent me off to my new married life with an old-fashioned shivaree. They came out to our farm honking horns and clanging on pans.

Donald and I were married for 71 years. I guess you could say it was another wise career choice.

STELLA KING WILSON
DICKENS, IA

The Stroudsmoor had room for up to 160 guests, most of them from New York City and Long Island. Fred worked 12-hour days, seven days a week, as part of the hotel waitstaff.

YOUR REFRESHMENT, SIR AND MADAM

SUMMERS DURING MY JUNIOR AND SENIOR years of high school in 1949 and '50 were spent working as a bellhop at the Stroudsmoor Hotel in Stroudsburg, Pennsylvania. I was only 16, and they would have preferred someone of college age, but they needed someone *now*. Plus I was tall for my age, and they must have believed I could carry luggage without difficulty. In addition to carting suitcases in and out, I delivered beverages to various locations on the property—to the rooms, tennis court, swimming pool or recreation area. I got room and board, plus $5 a week; tips averaged $60 to $65 a week.

Working those two summers gave me the people skills that proved invaluable throughout my career as a teacher, principal and eventually superintendent of schools.

FRED SERFASS
POTTSTOWN, PA

SMALL TALK WITH FRIENDS

A TALKER BY NATURE, MY MOTHER, Barbara Fleece, worked as a switchboard operator for Michigan Bell Telephone Co. in 1951 when she was 18. It was her first real job and she won an award for her outstanding work performance.

While there, my mom worked alongside one of her dearest lifelong friends, Jean Bradford. Often between customer service calls during their work shifts, they would connect to each other's control-board consoles and chat. Their supervisor eventually caught on to their ruse and split them up. As a result, Jean was assigned to a different area servicing long-distance calls, and Mom continued to work on local calls.

STAN FLEECE
TRAVERSE CITY, MI

Connecting calls for customers was Barbara's job, but it also gave her an outlet for her caring spirit.

Try the Meatball Sandwich

Mom knew a thing or two about Italian cooking.

Like all Italian mothers, my mom, Mae DiMarco, made the best spaghetti sauce in the world. But unlike the other moms, her sauce went public in front of Hollywood stars.

My dad had received two valuable food-stand franchises for the Los Angeles County Fair when it reopened in 1948. Prior to that, the location had served as a military camp and prisoner of war center during and after World War II. Dad decided to serve traditional hamburgers and hot dogs in one of the stands. In the other, he took a chance by serving lesser-known items— Italian sandwiches. One of them was a meatball sandwich dipped in pasta sauce. And whose meatballs and sauce would be better to serve than my mother's?

The sandwiches consisted of three meatballs smothered in Mom's delicious sauce and served on a tasty French roll. They were a big hit at the fair, the second-largest in the country. But in 1950, the sandwiches underwent a stiff taste test.

Ezio Pinza, the famous Metropolitan Opera basso, had undertaken the male lead in *South Pacific* when it opened on Broadway in 1949. The show, co-starring Mary Martin, became a megahit and introduced such songs as "Some Enchanted Evening" and "Bali Ha'i." After winning a Tony Award at 57, Pinza became a household name.

While in Hollywood to fulfill a movie contract with MGM, Pinza visited the fair. When my

Tony worked the food stand where his mom and dad introduced Italian sandwiches to fairgoers.

mother spotted him eyeing our sign with skepticism, she quickly made him a meatball sandwich free of charge. He took it and then disappeared.

A short while later, he returned, this time with an entourage of almost a dozen people. My mom asked, "*Ti è piaciuto?*" (Did you like it?)

A broad smile came over Pinza's face as he replied, "*Deliziosa!*"

He ordered a dozen sandwiches on the spot and later came back for more. It certainly was a fine endorsement but not a surprise for those of us who had enjoyed Mom's cooking for years.

How could Ezio Pinza not have liked her sauce? It was the best.

TONY DiMARCO
LOS ANGELES, CA

FUN FACTS

Ezio Pinza could not read music; he memorized every song.

....

Pinza spent 22 years with the New York Metropolitan Opera.

....

During a scene in the 1980 film *The Blues Brothers*, Pinza's voice is heard singing "*Anema e core.*"

HOOFING IT ON
THE BALLROOM FLOOR

BEING A TEENAGER DURING World War II in Hebron, a small town in central Ohio, presented a special employment opportunity for me and my contemporaries. Everyone just a few years older than us was either inducted into the service or employed by one of the defense plants that had cropped up. As a result, jobs not previously available to kids were ours for the asking.

Nearby was an amusement park called Buckeye Lake, also known as the Playground of Ohio. The park had a variety of rides, concessions, games and eateries, as well as a skating rink and two dance halls. The plethora of jobs there was amazing, and the laws covering child labor were much more relaxed than they are today.

I began working in 1944, when I was 14, at a dance hall, the Crystal Ballroom.

As the dance floor manager, I supervised 10 ticket takers, mopped and treated the dance floor with cornmeal and shaved paraffin, and set up music stands and microphones.

A house band was booked for the entire summer. However, big-name bands such as the Dorsey brothers, Benny Goodman, Harry James, Charlie Barnet, Gene Krupa and even Spike Jones made occasional appearances. We used the dime-a-dance ticket system with the house band. With big names, however, we charged a general admission fee but the dancing was free.

After each dance number, I hustled everyone off the dance floor. I also made sure that no one was inebriated and that the dancing didn't get excessively vigorous. The jitterbug was big and at times people overdid it.

We worked seven days a week from 7 p.m. until close at 1 a.m. Then we walked 2 miles home along a busy highway full of drivers who had been doing their fair share of drinking that night. I worked there for three years before joining the Navy when I turned 17.

There is no way parents would allow kids to do this today.

JOHN COOPERIDER
HOOKSETT, NH

In the late '20s, Jack worked on a crew installing power lines in Ohio. Steady work on utility crews meant Jack moved his family around a lot.

RETURNING THE FAVOR
My father, Jack LeRoy Unland, found work during the late 1920s and '30s throughout Ohio and Illinois installing telephone and electric lines, and farming during the Depression. In all those years I don't remember Dad ever saying anything derogatory about anyone. Nor did he and my mother argue in front of us kids. Dad was the kind of guy who picked up hitchhikers from Ohio State University, because other people had helped him when he needed a hand.

MAXINE THOMPSON · BRADENTON, FL

PASTEL REVOLUTION

Earl S. Tupper's "plastic of the future" and Brownie Wise's genius for selling it launched a marvel of the 20th century: Tupperware. The product transformed the American household, gave women new earning power and paved the way for today's shop-at-home lifestyle.

Kitchen Innovation
Early versions of Tupper's line were all white and sold at department stores. But sales were slow until a woman named Brownie Wise threw a party to show how bowls could actually bounce. The Plastic of the Future, as it was called, was trademarked as Poly-T by Tupper Plastics. It was marketed as being flexible and featherweight.

1970s

Rainbow of Food Storage

Burnt orange, avocado and gold were the dominant
Tupperware colors in the 1970s.

ALL IN A DAY'S WORK

My mom worked at the Starlite Dude Ranch Drive-In, Maryville, Missouri, in '64. She loved the job but hated wearing a cowboy hat because it messed up her beehive hairdo.

SHANNON SCHNEIDER
WAMEGO, KS

PICK A PECK

I was 15 when I got my first job in 1954 working at Sunnyside Farm Products in Affton, Missouri, near St. Louis. The farm stand's owner, Ray Knierim, employed teenage clerks and paid them 50 cents an hour. We worked so many hours, sometimes I made as much as my mom, who worked at the local bank.

JIM EYDMANN · GRANITE CITY, IL

ENOUGH FOR EVERYONE

Prep cooks in the cafeteria of Cockrill Elementary School in Nashville, Tennessee, ready food trays in this photo from the early 1940s. My mother-in-law, Jerdie Toler Garland (far right), worked there. Schools and church basements were often used as sites for fundraising meals. At that time, volunteers converged on the kitchens to whip up mass quantities of food.

MARIE MURPHY GARLAND · NASHVILLE, TN

While I was home from college, my summer job in 1969 was driving my scooter through neighborhoods in Rochester, New York, selling Skippy ice cream. I rang the bells and kids raced out to greet me.

DAVE SKIRVIN · INDIANAPOLIS, IN

After a bust, Charles Campbell, second from right, hides his .38-caliber revolver under his suit jacket after finding an illegal still in South Dakota.

Memories of an ATF Agent

Upholding the law before and after Prohibition.

My father, Charles E. Campbell, joined the Bureau of Prohibition, forerunner to the Bureau of Alcohol, Tobacco, Firearms and Explosives, in 1920 as a prohibition agent. After the 18th Amendment passed in 1919, the production and sale of alcohol was outlawed. The Volstead Act gave the federal agency power to enforce the law.

Although not a member of Eliot Ness' fabled Untouchables in Chicago, Illinois, my father nonetheless was in the second group of agents joining the agency, stationed in both Chicago and Omaha, Nebraska.

More than a decade later, after Prohibition was repealed, he continued as an agent stationed in Rapid City, South Dakota, sharing an office and a secretary with an FBI agent. In the late '40s and '50s, the crimes that justified federal intervention in western South Dakota included possessing automatic firearms, operating stills, and smuggling alcohol into the country without paying federal taxes.

One of the many stories my dad told involved a group of enterprising criminals who tried to sell Scotch whisky smuggled from Canada into Rapid City without paying the federal tax. With the help of an informant, Agent Campbell busted the criminals.

For his length of service and the outstanding number of arrests he made, my father received the Albert Gallatin Award. His name is displayed in the foyer of the U.S. Treasury Department in Washington, D.C.

CAL CAMPBELL
VENICE, FL

Homefront Volunteers

In 1943, women in white met monthly in the basement of the United Reformed Church
of Williamsbridge Road in the Bronx, New York, to roll bandages for medical hospitals overseas.
My mother-in-law, Anna Ahders, second row, second from right, volunteered for the cause.

JOAN AHDERS · NEW HARTFORD, NY

CHAPTER 6

....

OUR HEROES

They gave of themselves for freedom.
We honor their personal stories and
those from family members here.

They Made It Their Own

"Home is where you dig it" reads the sign over the fighting bunker
of privates from the 1st Battalion, 7th Marine Regiment,
during Operation Worth in Vietnam, March 1968.

Operation Big Switch

A soldier recounts the emotional exchange of prisoners
at the close of the Korean War.

W ith the signing of the armistice that ended the Korean War on July 27, 1953, I was sent to assist with the exchange of prisoners known as Operation Big Switch. Few today know about this phase of the conflict, but it affected some 87,000 troops on both sides.

Operation Big Switch involved the repatriation of soldiers and civilians who'd been taken captive during the fighting, including more than 3,000 Americans.

A few months before Big Switch began, a smaller swap of sick and wounded prisoners called Operation Little Switch occurred at the capital, Seoul. I had watched as helicopters, each with four wounded returnees, touched down in a clearing among Seoul's bombed-out buildings. Hundreds of Koreans lined the perimeter of the landing circle, with more seated on the surrounding rubble, all desperate to see a father, husband or son among the wounded.

The crowd was silent, the only sound coming from the rhythmic *swish* of the helicopter rotors. As soon as the aircraft grazed the ground, the crowd burst into a loud, brief cheer before falling

Left, wounded POWs land in Seoul, South Korea. Cpl. Fred Benton, below, witnessed the repatriation of Korean War prisoners.

silent again. Nothing I ever witnessed touched me as much as that.

Later, I reported to the 55th Replacement Company in the South Korean port city of Inchon, a repatriation site for Operation Big Switch. Helicopters were already delivering our returning soldiers. My heart beat fast as I saw the aircraft land, wait just long enough to allow passengers to disembark, then quickly take off again to retrieve more POWs.

I saw five repatriates exit a helicopter, duck to avoid the

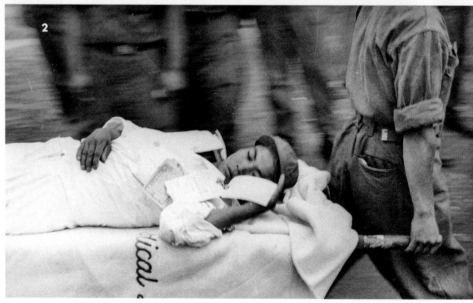

1. Freed prisoners hurry to get off the helicopter at Inchon, South Korea.
2. A wounded POW is carried off the chopper in Seoul.
3. Hundreds wait in silence during Operation Little Switch in Seoul, anxious to see a loved one.
4. A sign greets American POWs at Inchon during Operation Big Switch.

Some of these men had been in captivity since the first day of the war more than three years earlier.

swirling blades, and wave to the crowd. Those soldiers and other returning POWs got a hot shower, clean if ill-fitting fatigues, and some food before coming to us in the Counter Intelligence Corps for debriefing.

Our primary duty was to gather information about prisoners they knew weren't coming home, for whatever reason.

As we were explaining the procedure, several of the POWs struggled to hold up their heads. Some of these men had been in captivity since the first day of the war more than three years earlier.

A few had news about GIs reported as missing in action. Many of the MIAs had died of malnutrition, a disease such as malaria, dysentery or beriberi—or simply because they had lost the will to live. We filled out form after form. In quadruplicate.

On my last day, a colonel shuffled up to my table. Very thin and obviously ill, he sat motionless for several minutes before telling me he was an infantry division colonel and had been captured four days into the conflict.

He reached into a pocket for a mechanical pencil, holding it as if it were a precious jewel, and gently placed it on the table.

"Everything's right there," he said, instructing me to take the cap off and pull out the tube inside, but to do so carefully. "It damages easily."

Former POWs arrive in the U.S. at Pier 54 in San Francisco, California.

COMING HOME

The United Nations Command returned more than 1,000 Chinese and 5,000 Korean soldiers and about 450 civilians, while the communist side repatriated 684 UNC sick and wounded soldiers during Operation Little Switch, April 20 to May 3, 1953.

....

Operation Big Switch began Aug. 5, 1953, nine days after the armistice, and lasted until Dec. 23, 1953. It saw the repatriation of more than 87,000 POWs—about 12,000 UNC troops from the communists, and 75,000 Korean and Chinese soldiers from the UNC.

....

Some 20,000 captives, many of them Chinese Nationalists who supported exiled leader Chiang Kai-shek, refused to return to communist rule.

....

Prisoners on both sides who didn't want to go back to their home countries came under the care of a neutral nations commission for a short period. In time, many Chinese and Koreans were forced to repatriate anyway and faced persecution at home. A small number of former POWs were allowed to relocate elsewhere with help from the neutral commission.

I removed a 1-inch-wide cylinder of rice paper that was so tightly wound, it took some effort to loosen. Once it uncoiled, however, it stretched out more than 5 feet. On it were the names of 232 GIs who had died during the colonel's captivity, with rank, serial number and cause of death.

The thought of him carefully recording each name and protecting the list from the enemy for almost three years brought tears to my eyes. I stood and saluted him; I didn't know what else to do. Words would have been inadequate.

Hours later, the repatriates boarded the USS *General A.W. Brewster*, which was anchored offshore, for the final leg of their journey home.

Our reports from the debriefings were very vital to the War Department. The colonel and other captives had given the families of missing soldiers the gift of knowing what had happened to their loved ones and a chance to grieve their loss.

D. FRED BENTON
PORTLAND, OR

Back from the Abyss

Mother kept faith when faced with bad news.

——

My grandmother declared: "No, my Isaac is not dead. He will come home."

She was steadfast after receiving a letter from the U.S. War Department telling her that her son was missing in action and had been officially declared dead.

My uncle Isaac Laughrun was raised on a small farm in Yancey County, North Carolina. He joined the Army Air Corps in 1940 and, in October 1941, was sent to Corregidor in the Philippines, promoted to sergeant, and made a machine gunner.

By 1942, the Japanese had cut off supply lines to the island. Gen. Jonathan M. Wainwright along with a few thousand men occupying the island were forced to surrender.

After a three-week stay in a converted prison in Manila, Isaac was sent to Manchuria. As a POW, he worked seven days a week, sunrise to sunset. The prisoners were paid one yen per day for their labor (in today's money, 113 yen equals $1) and often bought food from the peasants to supplement their poor diets.

They walked 8 miles from the camp to a factory and, because the camp was 18 miles from the Siberian border, it was often 20 to 25 degrees below zero. Isaac found a GI blanket and, with cords taken from cement bags, he fashioned a coat to wear over his Japanese-issued uniform.

"The camp was far from escape-proof," he said, "but where would you go?"

Three men escaped but were recaptured and shot as their fellow POWs were forced to watch. "The Japanese possessed a knack for making life unbearable," Isaac added.

The prisoners barracks were made of wood slats with a dirt floor. Heat came from a single potbellied stove and one scuttle of coal rationed every 24 hours. It was not uncommon to be talking to a man before you went to sleep and find him dead when you awoke.

When Isaac had time alone, he wrote in his diary. One entry reads: "I hope God will bless us and deliver us home; I pray every night that this war will be over soon."

Isaac embraces his mother, Martha Laughrun, before shipping out to the Pacific.

And one day it was. Russians liberated the surviving POWs at Mukden prison camp Aug. 20, 1945. Isaac arrived home weighing 96 pounds, down from 146. A few months later he married his childhood sweetheart, and they had a daughter, Brenda. After 54 years home, he died in 2000.

Isaac believed the suffering that he and his fellow soldiers endured was worthwhile—the price of freedom.

DAVID PETERSON
JOHNSON CITY, TN

Above, a day's rickshaw ride in what was Tsingtao, China, cost Leo and his buddies Moe and Schwartz a mere 25 cents. The three friends also bought the struggling family a meal. At right, Leo is all smiles after his discharge in 1946.

One Hitch Was Enough

His wartime stint in the Navy served him well.

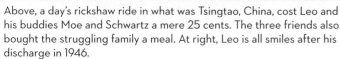

My father, Leo F. Gavlick, joined the Navy during World War II because all his friends were doing it. He was only 17 at the time and still in high school, so he had to wait for his assignment.

He chose the Navy because it meant he didn't have to sleep in the mud. But life on a ship was monotonous. Dad used to say, "They also serve who sit and wait"—and it well could have been the unofficial motto of his branch of the service.

In the war he served on the battle cruiser USS *Alaska* in the Pacific Theater. The *Alaska* took part in the battles of Okinawa and Iwo Jima, among others, where the ship saw action as a carrier escort. Dad witnessed firsthand the damage inflicted by kamikazes, the Japanese suicide pilots. He was a sight setter on the Quad 40, a 40 mm quadruple anti-aircraft gun, which might explain his postwar interest in pursuing education to become a civil engineer and surveyor.

Dad brought back a few souvenirs from the war, including a rifle (without the firing pin, of course) that he picked up from a pile confiscated from Japanese prisoners, and a Samurai sword he bought from a Marine who needed money for a poker game. He also got a strictly decorative Chinese sword from a street dancer.

It took many years before my father would talk about the war, but one highlight he liked to recount was dancing with Esther Williams, who he said was very tall. The future astronaut Wally Schirra was assigned to the ship for a short time. And Dad fondly recalled a stopover at Tsingtao (now Qingdao), China, where the Russian owners of a restaurant went out of their way to cook a Polish meal for him and his friends.

Though proud of his military service, Seaman Leo Gavlick knew, even at the tender age of 20, that one war was enough for one lifetime. He was honorably discharged in 1946.

BARBARA GAVLICK HARTNETT
SWOYERSVILLE, PA

WARTIME WORKERS

When companies recognized the efforts of those on the homefront.

Men Are Back

When this Chrysler ad appeared in *Life* in January 1945, the tide of war that had started shifting with D-Day the previous June infused the Allies with hope for victory. That meant soldiers would soon be coming home. This image anticipates the transition: Female workers still in their factory coveralls look up at men dressed to take their place.

« 1942

A Varied Effort

This lively ad from Heinz, long identified with its slogan "57 Varieties," features pictures of real women doing essential wartime jobs, from munitions assembly and inspection to engine repair to communications and navigation. The last image, an illustration, represents the ideal that all those women are working for and that service members are fighting for: a peaceful family meal, with ketchup (naturally).

HARTFORD HANGOUT
My mother, Loretta Godwin, is on the far left in this photo taken in 1943 at a USO dance in Hartford, Connecticut. She was 18. I'm grateful for this picture because I have so few of her in her youth, and it reflects the camaraderie of sailors and gals getting a break from the war.
CARLA BOLLINGER · NEWBURY PARK, CA

GROWING UP AS ARMY BRATS
George and I were born six minutes apart on April 3, 1925. I was the older sibling, but George always called me "little sis." We even had our own language. George fought in both World War II and Korea, where his plane was shot down on June 13, 1952. I will miss him always.
JOANNE PATTON THOMAS
SAN DIEGO, CA

BANDS OF BROTHERS, YOUNG AND OLD
In Vietnam, I strove as a first lieutenant to make friends, share traditions and safeguard connections to home.
RONALD RALEIGH
MACON, GA

1. Ron entertains kids from the local school. **2.** The 9th Infantry Division gave Ron a going-away party.
3. Ron used a crate bottom as a desk to write letters home. **4.** Officers' Club treats: MoonPies (not pictured) and RC Cola.

bathe out of a basin. It was a simple, easy life.

In Flagstaff, Arizona, we left the trailer at a gas station to drive down a narrow, rocky road to the Grand Canyon, which was breathtaking beyond description. We happened to park near a couple from Galesburg, Michigan, and we all hugged as if we knew each other.

In the mountains, we passed several big cars on the side of the highway with radiators boiling over. Our coupe was performing beautifully, thanks to Bob, a top-notch mechanic who kept the car well-tuned. I was proud.

The mountain driving involved a lot of maneuvering around tight corners and up and down steep grades, but we finally reached the foothills, where we could see miles of flat road leading into Bakersfield, California. As we descended, we continued to gain speed, until I peeked at the dashboard and saw that we were going 82 mph.

I gripped Bob's arm. "I don't like to go this fast," I told him.

"I don't either," he said. "But we have no more brakes." We had to ride it out as best we could.

At the end of our journey we settled in at a Culver City trailer park. Bob worked for the Flying Tigers for several months until the company relocated to Burbank. We couldn't find a decent trailer park near there, so we moved on. We traveled as far as Oregon in hopes of finding another airline job for Bob before eventually deciding to head back home to Michigan.

After a terrifying haul east through the mountains on switchback roads beside 6,000-foot drops, I'd had enough of that Kozy Coach. We sold it in Reno, Nevada, to a couple who planned to take it to Alaska along the recently built Alcan Highway. I wished them good luck and blew a kiss goodbye to what had been our sweet little home for over a year. We'd seen a lot of the country together.

FLORENCE SNOW FINKEY
KALAMAZOO, MI

THE ROOTS OF 66

America's first fully paved highway has a storied history.

Lt. Edward Beale, head of the U.S. Army Camel Corps, surveyed part of the route in 1857.

....

Established in 1926, it covers 2,448 miles.

....

Cyrus Avery of Tulsa, Oklahoma, oilman and loyal 66 booster, nicknamed it the Main Street of America.

....

An early 66 publicity stunt was the Bunion Derby, a 1928 footrace from California to New York. Cherokee runner Andy Hartley Payne won the $25,000 prize.

....

John Steinbeck called it "the mother road" in *The Grapes of Wrath*, his 1939 chronicle of Dust Bowl migrants.

....

It was decertified in 1985, but about 85 percent is still drivable.

The Kozy Coach rolled along behind the Snows' trusty 1940 Plymouth as they made their way down Route 66. The trailer was the couple's home for more than a year.

Then, as today, the stretch of Route 66 through Arizona is one of otherworldly beauty.

SHE FELT THE KICKS ON ROUTE 66

LIFE WAS HARD IN ARKANSAS IN 1925. There was no work; people were going hungry.

So my parents, Henry and Ollie King, decided to hitch up a wagon and, with their three children, head out on Route 66 for California, the land of plenty. All was going well until they reached the desert. Ollie shook her head.

"Turn around," she said, "or we'll all die of thirst in that desert."

So they headed back toward Bonnerdale, Arkansas, but on the way, they ran into another small snag: It seems my mother was expecting a baby. I was born in the covered wagon on Route 66 near Sapulpa, Oklahoma.

I now live in Mountain View, very close to Arkansas State Highway 66.

HERSHEL KING
MOUNTAIN VIEW, AR

Driven to roam Route 66 in my brand-spanking-new Pontiac ragtop, a friend and I traveled from Ohio to California—and back again—in the summer of 1948.
LOIS ANN "TAN" GRAHAM
LIMA, OHIO

A TIMELY TRIP

SETTING OUT BRIGHT AND early that day in February 1964, I was eager to begin my trip west. I had just graduated from Purdue University and looked forward to driving a new blue Ford Fairlane 500—my graduation present—from my home in Rockville, Indiana, to California, where I'd accepted a job.

In St. Louis, Missouri, I lost sight of the other car I'd been traveling with while navigating the construction zone around the base of the Jefferson National Expansion Memorial—now known more famously as the Gateway Arch—which wouldn't be completed until the next year. I was relieved to be on my own; now I could drive without the constant worry of keeping another car in my rearview mirror.

On day three, I got to Flagstaff, Arizona, about 5 p.m., checked into a motel and settled in to wait out a snowstorm. The next morning there were at least 10 cars in the ditch within the first few miles I drove. I cruised on by, glad that those fierce Hoosier blizzards had taught me something about how and when to drive in bad weather.

I reached Pasadena, California, as the sun set, the valley before me an expanse of multicolored lights. Never before had I seen anything so exotic—it struck fear into the heart of this Indiana farm girl.

But it was a good kind of fear, for California was my land of promise: My solo flight along the Mother Road had brought me to the home of Douglas Aircraft, where the next week I would start my career as an engineer in the science and space division.

SHARLIE WOIWOD
ARVADA, CO

Reed Lesiak of Addison, Illinois, snapped this Model A Ford at a historic gas station in 2014 while on an antique auto club trip to Pontiac, Illinois, along The Old Road.

FINDING HIS WAY

At 20, I took a break from college to escape a brutal Wisconsin winter. Inspired by the TV series *Route 66*, about two guys experiencing the mystique of the road in a Corvette, I set out in January 1963 on what turned into a four-year odyssey.

My 1955 Chevy held heat for only about an hour, so I plowed through the northern section as quickly as I could. In New Mexico, I went through downtown Albuquerque in late evening. As night gave way to daybreak, the grandest sight of my Route 66 experience was before me: the mountains. That view of sun-drenched peaks is one I'll never forget. I saw beauty even in the desolate stretches as the expanse of Arizona desert carried me westward.

For me, Route 66 was more than an adventure. It was my passage to adulthood.

DICK LARDINOIS · CRIVITZ, WI

The Mendillos made a mad dash for New Jersey along Route 66 one Christmas.

Eastward Ho!

A holiday rush to the other coast.

Angel and I married in 1951, and shortly afterward I was drafted into the Army and assigned to the Presidio of San Francisco, California. We lived off post until I got my orders for Korea on Dec. 19, 1952. I had furlough until Jan. 3, so we decided to go home to New Jersey for the holidays.

We bought a used car and loaded it up. I had thought ahead and bought chains in case we encountered snow. That was the smartest thing I did, as we hit a storm at Tehachapi Pass in the Sierra Nevada mountains. Cars were sliding all around me, but I was able to stay on the road.

We had only a blanket to keep us warm. I wanted to drive straight through to make it in by Dec. 25, but we were so cold that in New Mexico I stopped to have a car heater installed. After that, the biggest danger was that I'd fall asleep at the wheel. We'd pull over for quick catnaps, and the rest of the time Angel recited nursery rhymes to keep me awake.

Meanwhile, the car burned oil. Whenever I topped it up I had to keep it running or it wouldn't start again until the motor cooled. I'd forget and have to flag someone for a push. We were lucky—people always helped.

We got home at 1:30 a.m. on Dec. 26—but it was 10:30 p.m. Christmas night, California time. So technically, we made it!

ALAN MENDILLO · WAYNE, NJ

RAISED ON THE ROAD

Route 66 is truly my Mother Road. I grew up in Fontana, then Azusa, and as an adult, I lived in Glendora—all on Route 66 in California. I married my husband, Ted, in 1960 at St. Frances of Rome Church on Route 66 in Azusa. It's still there and always packed on Sundays. Throughout the '60s and '70s, I worked at several businesses along Route 66, including a thrift store, a grocery, a boat dealer and the Foothill Drive-In Theatre in Azusa. They've all closed, although the Foothill's marquee is intact and the drive-in is sometimes used for special events.

I might add that I got my only traffic violation on Route 66. The officer who issued me the ticket turned out to be one of my neighbors.
KAREN MEYERS · TWENTYNINE PALMS, CA

When my car broke down near Roy's, I didn't have enough for the repairs, so I offered my wedding rings. I had to save up, but later I did return with the cash and got my rings back.

ANNE STANBROOK
SAN CLEMENTE, CA

ROY'S

NO VACANCY

MOTEL

CAFE

Roy's Cafe and Motel in Amboy, California, is one of the most recognizable sights along old U.S. 66. Built in 1938 and expanded in the '50s, Roy's angled storefront and Googie-style sign have appeared in dozens of films and TV shows.

Excellent Airport Adjoining
U.S. HIGHWAY 66 . . . Telephone #3 . . . AMBOY, CALIF.

ROY'S
CAFE
MOTEL

DRIVE
SCENIC U S
66

Paul's GOAT looked sharp when it was new in 1967 (above) and still looks fabulous today (right).

Ride of a Lifetime

He relives his carefree youth every time he gets behind the wheel.

After graduating from Miami University in Oxford, Ohio, in 1967, I purchased this Pontiac GTO brand-new. I was 21 and bought it because it looked cool. I figured that if the girls didn't like me, they'd at least like my car.

It cost about $3,350 at a time when I earned $93 a week as an accountant. It came with a 400-cubic-inch, 255-horsepower engine; automatic transmission; power steering; bucket seats; and Firestone redline tires. I added the Rally II wheels later.

Back in the mid-1970s, when American automakers stopped production on most convertibles, I decided I had better hold on to this original muscle car. I have never raced or modified it—or had any

accidents with it. With 124,000 miles, my GTO is essentially a survivor with the original interior, chassis and factory-applied Regimental Red paint.

I drove it every day for 10 years to the high school where I taught business and marketing. I'm retired now after 35 years as a teacher, but occasionally I'll meet former students who ask me if I still have that red car.

The old GOAT (the car, not me) turned 50 last year and still looks remarkable. I tell people that the GTO is part of my youth. How many baby boomers still have the car they drove on dates back in their 20s?

PAUL MEYER · DAYTON, OH

Neon Aglow

Blue Swallow Motel, still family-owned, has been a Tucumcari,
New Mexico, fixture since the 1940s. Retro enthusiasts love its pink
stucco exterior, period furnishings and groovy neon sign.

CHAPTER 8

SEEING STARS

Remember the celebrities who influenced
the decades, and enjoy recollections
of starstruck encounters.

King of Swing

In a late 1930s movie appearance, Benny Goodman wails on his clarinet
while the orchestra follows his lead, rousing audiences
with a mix of Big Band jazz and swing.

A Day in Her Life

Starstruck fan puts her skills to work for her idol.

———

After seeing Doris Day in *Calamity Jane* when I was 10, I was hooked and determined to meet the lovely lady with the gorgeous smile and beautiful voice. I even started networking before it was a thing, eager to find other Doris Day fans.

Thanks to *Photoplay* magazine, I joined the only official Doris Day Fan Club, based in London, England. Through the club, I met other fans—Eileen, Hilda and Mary—who lived in the Los Angeles area. We became friends and kept in touch via letters and phone calls. My parents questioned why our phone bills were so high with calls to the West Coast. My plan was one day to travel there, meet my new friends and, with luck, see and meet Doris Day, too.

I made my first pilgrimage to Los Angeles on Aug. 15, 1965, by myself. Ironically, it was at the height of the Watts riots, and my parents were not thrilled that I had such a one-track mind. But I was determined to go.

Once in Los Angeles, I met my "Day Gang" buddies, but our efforts to meet Doris proved fruitless, despite driving past her Beverly Hills home countless times. Undeterred, I returned the following year. Again, no Doris.

By this time I'd graduated from Marian University in Indianapolis, majoring in English and journalism, and I'd landed a job as a reporter and feature writer for my home state *Indianapolis News*.

Persistent fans, my California friends eventually met Doris and told her I was making my third trip to Los Angeles and would love to meet her. Doris agreed, but no date or time was specified until finally, on Oct. 21, 1967, the day before I was to fly home to Indianapolis, my dream came true. Doris rode her bike to Bailey's Bakery, a local shop she frequented almost daily when she wasn't working, and met us for breakfast. I went into full reporter mode, asking about her next movie, her next record and more. Gracious, she answered every question, enjoying my enthusiasm.

I found Doris very down-to-earth, and we chatted like old friends. I told her that I wanted to move to the area; she encouraged the idea.

Much to my parents' chagrin, the following March I moved to Los Angeles, where my friend Mary and I lucked out by finding an apartment one block from Beverly Hills and within biking distance of Bailey's Bakery.

Mary and I looked forward to Saturdays when we would bike to the shop and have breakfast with Doris. We were thrilled when we saw her bicycle parked outside. Doris would visit with us, treating us like sisters and confiding about her TV show and her 11 dogs.

Soon after moving, I landed a job in public relations with The May Co. Then, on April 20, 1968, one month after I moved to the area, Doris' husband, Marty Melcher, died unexpectedly.

Bailey's Bakery, Doris and Mary Anne's frequent hangout, was a great place to discuss the issues of the day.

Doris' nickname for Mary Anne was Mairzy Doats, after a popular 1940s song Doris sang to her.

A few months later, the phone rang. It was Doris asking if Mary and I would meet her for breakfast at the farmers market and go shopping with her. We knew then that our friendship had gone beyond just being fans and a star.

A year later, I was in a car accident and broke both legs and my right arm. I was on disability for several months and, during my recovery, Doris and her mother, Alma, kept in touch with me.

While recuperating and before going back to work, I visited with Doris at Bailey's, our favorite hangout. At one point Doris said, "I'll bet you'd be a good secretary."

Two days after I went back to work, Doris called and asked me a single question: "How would you like to come work for me?"

I jumped at the chance, of course.

Every weekday I drove to her house, where her driver picked us up at 6:30 a.m. and took us to the CBS lot in Studio City to film *The Doris Day Show*. We always took three or four of her dogs with us. My duties varied. I was personal secretary, fan-mail response writer, dog walker, errand runner and assistant on many projects.

Then, two weeks before Christmas 1972, Doris' housekeeper abruptly left. Doris' mom had already made plans to spend the holidays with her family in Texas, so Doris would be alone. Knowing she would be overwhelmed, I volunteered to stay with Doris through the holidays. The housekeeper never returned, so those two weeks turned into almost two years.

My mother and friends back in Indianapolis were overjoyed that I got to live my dream.

Sounds like something that could happen only in the movies, right?

MARY ANNE BAROTHY · INDIANAPOLIS, IN

When he was 11 years old, Ron noticed that the Bradys lived in a cool house.

That's the Way He Became
The Brady Bunch

The '70s-era show left its mark.

From about 1970 to 1973, I must have watched every episode of *The Brady Bunch*, not because I loved the show, but because on Fridays it came on before *The Partridge Family*, which was my favorite. I waited excitedly through the chronicles of the Brady kids to see what David Cassidy and his rockin' family were up to each week.

Looking back, though, I've come to recognize that aside from their music, the Partridges had little influence on me, while the Bradys have shaped me in all sorts of ways.

I yearned for the Bradys' California sun, fancying myself a landlocked beach boy separated from his spiritual home. The large lots, green lawns and wide streets where the Bradys lived cemented in my mind the picture of the perfect neighborhood.

I was equally taken with the look of the Brady house—big backyard, flat driveway, carport with basketball hoop, and the open space inside, with floating staircase, exposed brick walls and artwork. Years later, I adopted a similar decor in my home, one free of clutter and with plenty of art for color. I even wound up with a Brady-style car, a 1970 Plymouth Barracuda.

Just as influential were the storylines. Some reflected my life—Peter overcoming his fear of the school bully, Buddy Hinton, for instance, or Greg resisting the pressure from his bandmates to smoke cigarettes.

Some episodes involved writing, which became my profession. It must have left an impression on me when Carol Brady wrote an article about her family for *Tomorrow's Woman* magazine. Like Carol, I saw value in the seemingly mundane and wrote about it, often seeing my work published. In another episode, Marcia composed an essay for a newspaper's Father of the Year contest. Following her lead, I wrote tributes to both of my parents that also made it into print.

Critics have bashed the show for being facile, but the truth is *The Brady Bunch* was ahead of its time in many ways, especially in its celebration of the blended family.

Watching the show now is like paging through a photo album. Familiar images bring back thoughts and feelings I'd long forgotten, and remind me where my ideas and aspirations originated. It's no wonder that I continue to enjoy *The Brady Bunch*. And I'm happy to be under its influence still.

RON BAXENDALE II
BROOMFIELD, CO

The Brady Bunch kids in 1969: Susan Olsen (Cindy), Maureen McCormick (Marcia), Christopher Knight (Peter), Barry Williams (Greg), Eve Plumb (Jan) and Mike Lookinland (Bobby).

Driving west, their shiny black car transported the family—from left, Maude, Walter, Patricia and Margaret—to California.

Can Curly Top Come Out to Play?

When in California, find out where the stars live.

The Dust Bowl and the Great Depression were two good reasons to leave Ardmore, Oklahoma, in June 1934. I was only 4 but I remember being tucked into bed with the covers pulled over my head and told to stay put while my mother, Maude, lined the windowsills with wet towels. Many who lost their jobs headed to California.

My dad, Walter, a newspaperman, had no trouble finding a job wherever we lived. A friend of his had gone to Alameda, California, and wrote back saying there was an opening for a pressman on the *Alameda Times-Star*.

My mother and my sister Margaret, 16, were thrilled about the move. California was where the movie stars lived, and Mother especially loved Shirley Temple and Mary Pickford.

Daddy bought a new used car. Mother packed and we waved goodbye to the neighbors. Daddy drove with my black kitten clinging to his shoulder. Mother sat in the front giving directions. My sister and I sat in the back singing "California, Here I Come" and "On the Good Ship Lollipop" all the way there.

When we reached Southern California, Daddy was tired and wanted to find a place to sleep. But Mother had a different idea. She bought a map from a gas station to find out where Shirley Temple lived, and soon we were parked in front of the star's home. To our surprise, it was just an ordinary-looking house in an ordinary neighborhood.

Mother told me to knock on the front door and ask if Shirley could come out and play. I did as I was told and a tall young man opened the door. He called out, "Mom, a little girl wants to play with Shirley!"

And what do you know? Down the stairs came Shirley Temple, her blond curls bouncing. She came right outside to where I was standing with her brother.

Then Mrs. Temple came out to say hello. At that point my mother and sister got out of the car and started talking with Mrs. Temple, while Shirley and I stared at each other as little kids do. Daddy stayed in the car with my kitten, wishing he could get back on the road and find a place to sleep.

PATRICIA GRIPON WALDRON
REDDING, CA

FUN FACTS

Shirley Temple went from child star to diplomat as a U.S. ambassador to Ghana and Czechoslovakia.

Born: April 23, 1928

············

Died: Feb. 10, 2014

············

Children: Three; a son and two daughters

············

Films include:
Little Miss Marker 1934
Now I'll Tell 1934
Bright Eyes 1934
Curly Top 1935
Poor Little Rich Girl 1936
Wee Willie Winkie 1937
Heidi 1937

My husband, Eldon, was 3 on July 4, 1941,
shortly before America joined the war.
Patriotism was strong at the time.

E.M. "COOKIE" MILLER
YELM, WA

Not at All the Great Pumpkin, Charlie Brown

This Halloween stinks!

My twin sister, Tracey, and I were 4 and our sister Margaret was 6 when we posed for a photograph (below) on Halloween 1967. Our sister was dressed as Casper the Friendly Ghost while Tracey and I wore the hobo masks that I am sure my mother bought at the dime store. With six children, my parents didn't have a lot of money for costumes. Every Halloween my mother got out those masks, and Tracey and I had to wear them if we wanted to go out trick-or-treating. Every year.

And every year we collected our Halloween candy in big paper bags from the grocery store. The one notable exception occurred in 1975. We were 12 and, yes, still using those hobo masks, but that year my mother had bought a plastic jack-o'-lantern to hold the candy she would pass out to trick-or-treaters. I begged her to let me use it instead so I wouldn't have to collect my treats in a paper bag. I whined and fussed profusely until I finally got my way.

I was so proud to carry that jack-o'-lantern door to door as I shouted smugly, "Trick or treat!" My sisters made fun of my self-importance and kept running ahead, leaving me behind.

They're just jealous, I thought.

They ran over some railroad tracks into a neighborhood we didn't know that well. I was struggling to keep up, yelling out, "Hey, you guys, wait for me!" when I tripped over a lawn sprinkler. As I went down, the cheap plastic strap on the jack-o'-lantern snapped off. My precious pumpkin head full of treats was suddenly spinning wildly through the air, candy shooting out over the grass like sparks from a twirling firecracker. I grabbed the broken jack-o'-lantern and frantically scooped up my treats, pleading with my sisters to help me.

Could this get any worse? I wondered.

Unfortunately, the answer was yes. I sniffed my hands and discovered that I'd been scooping up dog poop with my candy! My sisters laughed and ran away as I remained on my knees, now desperate to get my hands clean. My whole Halloween had turned into a smelly mess.

Later that night, my mother made my sisters share their candy with me, which they did grudgingly, giving me the second-rate stuff that no one likes.

My beloved jack-o'-lantern had let me down. Halloween was never the same again.

Teresa and Tracey always wore hobo masks on Halloween. Older sister Margaret went as Casper.

TERESA STANLEY • TULARE, CA

PICTURES *from the* PAST

COSTUMED KIDS

HORSING AROUND

As an amateur photographer, I took hundreds of slides of my family through the 1960s and 1970s. In this picture taken in 1964, my two children dressed up as a stallion for a special event.

BRUCE THOMPSON
WAUKESHA, WI

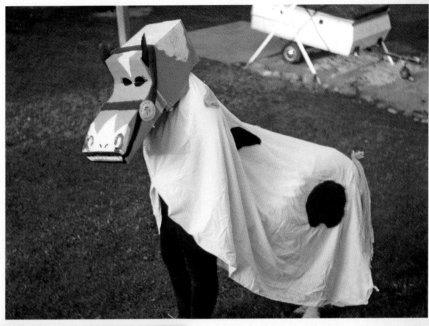

SNAP, CRACKLE, POP!

For every Halloween parade in Bellefonte, Pennsylvania, our mother, Barbara Korman, made us costumes based on a threesome theme. Jeff (left), Jack (right) and I won silver dollars each year. Here we are in 1964.

JOYCE WILKES
EDINBORO, PA

KITCHEN CARVER

Holiday tradition in our house meant that I carved the turkey. Here, getting directives from my wife, Joyce, I buzz into the bird with an electric knife—state-of-the-art equipment in 1965.
BRUCE THOMPSON · WAUKESHA, WI

When I was growing up in the '40s, my mother always made Thanksgiving dinner for my grandparents. While she prepared the meal, my dad took me and my brother to see the Thanksgiving Day parade in downtown Detroit, Michigan, which ended with Santa Claus waving to the crowds.

GEORGIA BROWNE · STURGIS, MI

UP NORTH IN THE PINK STATION WAGON

AUTOMOBILES TODAY ARE a marvel of technology and ingenuity. But I was raised during a simpler time. We had one car— a large pink Oldsmobile station wagon. The car wasn't awarded to us by Mary Kay but rather was chosen by my father out of necessity. Despite the color, the car had to haul five children and their parents all around western Minnesota, with holiday trips to visit grandparents in northern Minnesota.

The Olds had no seat belts, no air bags, no rear cameras and no warning alarms. We could count on two minimally effective safety features: 1. The car was built like a large pink tank, and 2. My mother.

With her maternal urge to protect her flock from head-on crashes, deer suddenly darting across the road, and the Russians unleashing the Big One on Middle America, my mother developed her own safety feature called "Hit the floor."

Although we never had to use it in an actual emergency, we practiced it frequently on trips to the Iron Range. There were no electronics involved, just the no-nonsense tone of Mom's voice yelling, "Hit the floor!"

No matter who was on your lap, who called shotgun or who had the enviable position by the window, five children, ranging in age from 2 to 14, dove for the floorboards, hoping to not be the one left on top to face the impending disaster. After all, we were still children and the world revolved around us.

I often wonder if our mom's strategy for using this device had another purpose on those seemingly endless trips to our grandparents' homes. Five antsy kids, packed in a car for three hours, would make a natural plot for a really scary movie. With parents on their last nerve, sisters bickering about the little brother touching them, the kids not having enough space to spread out, and one or more of us being hungry, tired or thirsty, the clamor eventually became too much to bear, and Mom would yell, "Hit the floor!"

All petty bickering stopped instantly as we scrambled for the floorboards, wondering what would happen next. The Olds was quiet while we awaited word to get back in our seats.

One time I peeked at Mom, who had a smirk on her face, and noticed a grateful nod from Dad, whose neck was red and pulsing.

When the Olds pulled into the driveway, all four doors flew open and, as if the car were a disturbed anthill, its occupants poured out. The fleeting look of panic on our grandparents' faces was soon replaced by smiles, hugs and kisses. Then we nearly knocked them over, racing inside to see what graced the dining table. Sure enough, a golden, magazine-worthy turkey, mounds of mashed potatoes, luscious brown gravy and a sideboard piled high with pies were enough to appease everyone.

SHERI SMITH
PONSFORD, MN

TO MARKET, TO MARKET, TO BUY A FAT TURKEY

ON THE TUESDAY BEFORE Thanksgiving 1932, Grandfather, Mother, my cousin Jack and I went on a special shopping trip in Oakland, California—not just down to East 14th Street, but all the way downtown to the big farmers market below 10th and Broadway.

Off we went, Jack and I running and hopping, down the street to catch good ol' No. 11. The trolley car came clanking and banging down the hill and hissed to a stop at our corner. We scrambled up the steps and Grandfather put four trolley tokens in the glass holder for all of us.

The motorman stomped his foot on the warning bell and, with his right hand, pulled the lever that snapped the doors shut. With a jerk and a start, the trolley zoomed down the hill.

Grandfather knew the motorman, so when the car wasn't crowded he stood and talked with him for a short time, bracing himself against the brass rail. I was glad when he sat down. A sign read: "All passengers MUST be seated when the trolley is in motion," and my cousin told me Grandfather could get in trouble if he didn't sit down.

I loved to ride the trolley! Our car, Trolley No. 11, sped along, careening around curves and slowing down as it went up the side of a hill. We whizzed past the movie house, Montgomery Ward, the hospital, assorted shops and the shores of Lake Merritt.

At last we passed the courthouse and rounded the corner. There was the Tribune Tower, for many years the tallest building around. It had a clock that could be seen for miles when it was lit up at night. Just as we passed the tower, Grandfather reached up and pulled the cord, and the trolley ground to a screeching stop. We scrambled off in a hurry.

The farmers market was big, and I never really liked it much. I was always afraid I'd get lost. There were huge open archways with iron gates to close them off at night. The tile floor was nearly always damp from being hosed down. Stalls for vegetables and fruit lined one wall. Cut flowers and potted plants ran along another wall. Down the center stood counters and places to buy drinks and food. At the far end of the market were the fish, chicken, rabbit and turkey sellers.

On our first stop, Grandfather picked out a turkey from a truckful out back. He looked over the birds carefully and pointed to the one he deemed best. He made arrangements to have it dressed and delivered to the house early the next day.

Then we went to the fish market. That was more fun because it didn't smell as bad. There were bins full of crabs crawling all over each other and waving their claws. There were big fish, little fish, squid with their odd-looking tendrils, and baskets of oysters and shrimp. Grandfather always picked out one—a large crab, some shrimp or oysters—but never all three.

The next stop was the fruit and vegetable stalls for fresh cranberries, pearl onions, and cauliflower or Brussels sprouts.

ILLUSTRATIONS: EDWIN FOTHERINGHAM

At a dairy stall, we bought butter and cream. The bags were full now and it was time to go— but not before Grandfather bought some good white wine. My mother bought some peppermints and perhaps a few apples or an orange or two. Mother and Grandfather each carried black leather shopping bags, now bulging and heavy.

We forged our way through the throngs of people. The marketplace was noisy, with everyone shouting to make themselves heard. Children were everywhere. Big sisters with baby brothers and bright-eyed boys,

noses pressed against the glass counters of pastries and candies.

There seemed to be people of every ethnicity and age: ancient Chinese gentlemen in long garments with beards, middle-aged Chinese women in black jackets and slippers with big pins in their hair, Swedish sailors with watch caps, and Italians and Portuguese. Grandfather spoke Portuguese, Italian and Swedish.

Soon we were boarding the No. 11 for the trip home.

Wednesday morning the pies were made, and Jack and I polished the silver. Then we folded napkins and did

other chores to keep us busy. The table was set and the centerpiece arranged. One year it was a horn of plenty, another year an Indian canoe with flowers. We made place cards using walnut shells with little sails for names.

In those days, schools closed for the week of Thanksgiving, allowing people to be with their families for a longer period of time or to travel to one another's homes, if necessary. The holiday was truly an event.

MAE ELIZABETH LOCKWOOD
OAKLAND, CA

Rolling Through the Years

Many hands make short work
of treasured ravioli recipe.

———

My mom and dad started the tradition of making raviolis more than 50 years ago, with my brother, sister and me helping out. We always made them on Christmas Day. After getting up early and opening our presents, we'd march into the kitchen and start the preparations for the special meal. Sometimes, as soon as we finished cleaning up, the doorbell would ring, announcing our company.

For a few years we made raviolis one week for Dad's family and the next week for Mom's family, but that didn't last very long—it was too much work. We just invited both sides of the family for one big meal.

The family recipe came from my maternal grandmother, Mary Saccaro, who learned it from her mother. The recipe had been handed down from mother to daughter for many generations in Sicily and carried over to Chicago, Illinois, when Grandma Saccaro's family arrived in the late 19th century.

Grandma never measured anything; it was all done by intuition. The recipe wasn't even written down until the early 1960s, when Grandma was making raviolis one last time to celebrate the birth of a granddaughter, and there was a danger we would lose the knowledge. My mother and several of my aunts measured and recorded the amounts whenever Grandma called for "a pinch" of this and "a handful" of that. When we tried the recipe the following year, we agreed the raviolis were as good as Grandma's had been.

Before we started the pasta, Mom made a red sauce of canned tomatoes, garlic, basil and oregano. She added Italian sausage, pork neck bones and homemade meatballs. Our sauce—we never called it "gravy," as the characters on *The Sopranos* referred to tomato sauce—simmered for hours; we basked in the aroma while we labored over the raviolis.

We sat around the kitchen table in an assembly line, flattening and turning the dough balls with the rolling pin. We'd fill the flattened dough with cheese, seal the dumplings with a shot glass, and crimp the edges with a fork.

Anyone who needed a break would take the finished raviolis from the kitchen table to the drying sheet in the bedroom, keeping a running tally of our production.

We never rolled out the dough with a pasta machine when I was a kid; we did it by hand to get the consistency just right. Everybody took turns with the rolling pin because it was a hard job. You could get fired or demoted if your rolling method wasn't up to Mom's standards. I should know—I've been demoted several times.

The yearly task of ravioli-making became a time to bond as we told stories about all the relatives and teased each other about past cooking mistakes. Nothing interfered with the process. Two weeks after my dad died, we still gathered in the kitchen, and making the raviolis helped us get through the grief as a family.

Over the years, spouses and grandchildren have joined the crew. We've also gotten high-tech: Now we grate the cheese with a hand-crank grater—no more skinned knuckles!—and start the flattening of the dough balls with a pasta machine, though we still finish rolling them by hand.

Today we make the raviolis a week in advance and freeze them, instead of getting up early on Christmas Day, but Mom still makes sure we follow Grandma Saccaro's original recipe to the letter. Our raviolis are as tasty as they were when we began the tradition.

FRANK C. MODICA
URBANA, IL

HELPING HANDS
We all did our part to help our grandma Lillian Stawarky fix the feast. We polished pans, mashed turnips and potatoes, and made cookies out of leftover pie crust. After dinner, we went downtown to see the holiday lights. My dad, Vin, took this photo in 1963. I'm third from the left in the back.
MIKE SIMKO
BRIDGEPORT, CT

MASTER DECORATORS
I fondly recall holiday baking with my kids Susan and Danny. Danny is sprinkling a paintbrush, which he used to decorate the cookies. This picture was taken in 1954 at our family's home in Madison, Wisconsin.
KAY SCHOPP · TUCSON, AZ

Multiple Layers of Paint

This cherished heirloom has survived five generations.

———

My mother, Marjorie Martin Mangrum, was from a family in Williamson County, Tennessee. Her grandfather B.C. Wilkes was a woodworker and made beautiful caskets and custom cabinetry.

In the fall of 1928, when my mom was 7, she visited her grandfather's workshop. She watched as he lovingly built a pint-sized china cabinet. She later told me how she wished that cabinet could be hers.

Her grandfather told her it was for a little girl who lived down the road. Imagine my mother's delight when she found the miniature piece of furniture under the Christmas tree that year.

Fast-forward to Christmas morning 1950. I found the same cabinet with a fresh coat of paint under our Christmas tree. My baby sister was born that year, and we spent countless happy hours playing house with our grown-up kitchen cabinet.

In 1966 and 1969, I had my own daughters. I replaced the cabinet's knobs and repainted it so my girls could use the piece in their playhouse.

My daughters had girls of their own, and every time they visited Granny's house, the first thing they wanted to play with was the little cabinet.

Now I have a great-granddaughter, Makayla, and whenever she stays with me she has a fun time playing outside with the storage unit she calls her kitchen.

I'm sure B.C. Wilkes never dreamed that five generations of little girls would continue the tradition of playing with the petite piece he built with love so many years ago.

Christmas 1950 brought Melba, top, plenty of fun playthings. Melba's great-granddaughter, Makayla, above, keeps up the family tradition.

MELBA BROWN
OLMSTEAD, KY

AN ADVERTISING VETERAN

Though St. Nick appeared in ads in 1840, it wasn't until after 1863, when cartoonist Thomas Nast created the now-familiar figure in a red suit with a white beard, that Santa became the holiday season's most popular pitchman.

1972 »

Yule Love This Salesman

In this ad from *Better Homes & Gardens*, Santa pitches the Sweet Story Book as a last-minute "life saver."

≈ 1962

Santa Suds

In *Family Circle*, Colgate's Soaky Santa bath suds was a popular stocking stuffer, and a toy when the bottle was empty.

« 1962

Kris Kringle Cold Calls

From *Family Circle*, Santa gives everyone's favorite condiment—long before Del Monte conceded to calling it ketchup in the '80s.

THE JOY OF CHRISTMAS

NONSTOP SMILE

Here I am as a 6-year-old, hugging a doll on Christmas morning 1956 while showing off my gappy grin. Only eight years earlier, Spike Jones and His City Slickers recorded "All I Want for Christmas Is My Two Front Teeth," which became a Billboard hit and has remained a popular holiday novelty song all these years. Several artists have recorded their own version, including George Strait, Nat King Cole and Jimmy Buffett.
LYNETTE JEAN GIBBONEY
COLUMBUS, OH

THE BIG HAUL

In December 1960, a friend and I paid $2 for a pair of pines we cut ourselves at a Michigan farm, and then we drove back to Chicago. We must have looked like a bush going down the highway in my '57 Chevrolet.
WARREN KOSTELNY · MOUNT PROSPECT, IL

GRATEFUL KIDS

What's Christmas without a fireplace, even if it is cardboard? My children, from left, Kevin, Gregory, Paula and Kathleen, show off their Christmas gifts in 1966.

BARBARA MOHR
MILLINGTON, MI

CHRISTMAS CAME AT LAST

Our military family lived in Germany and was scheduled to return to America in December 1954. Mom had shipped our Christmas gifts to our grandparents' house in Evansville, Indiana. But our return was delayed, and my younger brother, David, 4, and I worried that Santa would never find us. Mom bought us a few small presents and made us picture books of all the things Santa had delivered to Indiana. When we finally arrived in February, our grandparents Vernie and Stella Jones (above) had a fully decorated tree waiting for us. We had the best Christmas ever.

ROBERTA SHARP · MOORESVILLE, IN

SANTA'S SECRET

Even though I could not speak English then (1945), I was so excited to see Sani Closi, as we called him in Italian, in Santa Cruz, California.

NORMA WILSON
SCOTTS VALLEY, CA

Celebrating Grandma's birthday in 1949, Arlene sits with her doll and Grandma Elizabeth Scott.

All Aglow in Lights

Grandma's birthday was the final hurrah.

Little Christmas, also known as Epiphany, was nearly as special as Christmas when I was growing up in the 1940s in Iron River, Michigan. On Jan. 6, all my relatives got together to celebrate my grandmother's birthday and take down her Christmas tree with her. Sometimes my aunts, uncles and cousins from as far as Marquette, Michigan (almost 90 miles away), would come for a visit.

We cousins were allowed to carefully remove the special ornaments from the tree. I remember them well, especially two wooden Easter eggs given to Grandma by a neighbor girl who went to college— a big deal in our small town. Grandma tied ribbons around them and turned them into ornaments.

The ornaments were carefully wrapped in tissue paper and packed in a box that was stored behind a curtain in Grandma's closet until the week before Christmas the following year. In those days, we never put up decorations any earlier than a week before Christmas. It just wasn't right.

Some years I helped Grandma make paper chains from construction paper to decorate the tree (those we threw away). Once, we made popcorn-and-cranberry chains, but we didn't try that again because it was too hard to run the needle and thread through the popcorn without breaking it and pricking our fingers.

Taking Grandma's special sugar cookies off the tree was the best part of the event. By early January the cookies were pretty stale, but to us kids they were still delicious. We felt very grown up eating cookies and drinking coffee with the adults. Of course, our coffee was diluted with canned milk and sugar.

Uncle John also bought a special birthday cake at the A&P store. Grandma couldn't be expected to bake her own birthday cake.

We sat in her living room, turned on the tree lights and basked in their glow one last time, enjoying the stale Christmas cookies, store-bought birthday cake and coffee.

The final step was to remove the lights from the tree. It was always a little sad being tucked into bed that night, knowing it wouldn't be Christmas again for another whole year.

But that wasn't the end. The next morning my uncles hauled Grandma's tree outdoors, where my older cousins and their friends placed it on the hill and covered it with snow. Their makeshift ski jump lasted until about March, when the snow melted.

ARLENE SHOVALD · SALIDA, CO

Joyous Noel

In 1960, the year I turned 5, my family celebrated Christmas in
Karlsruhe, Germany, where my father, Gabby, an engineer, worked for
the Singer sewing machine company. My older sister, Phyrne, 13, loved
stuffed animals as much as I did. My mom, Fernanda, took the photo.

PHYLLIS GEBHARDT · KISSIMMEE, FL

CHAPTER 10

LAST LAUGH

Who doesn't love a good laugh?
Delight in these silly situations and good
fun—after all, a smile is universal.

Be a Clown

Members of the Mills Bros. Circus, this clown troupe
traveled from the East Coast to the Midwest with a stop
in Janesville, Wisconsin, on July 3, 1950.

Dressed for church, from left, are Dede's mom, Ellen Marston, sister Polly and her mother-in-law, Mabel Wilson.

Oh, She Can Help You

Look-alike servers confuse the congregation.

The Rev. Franklin Parker (a legend among area folks) and his wife, our Aunt Al, were host and hostess for the Saturday evening Baked Bean Suppers sponsored by the Chichester Congregational Church in Chichester, New Hampshire, many years ago.

When we were teenagers, my sister, Polly, and I often pitched in and waited on tables. In spite of a three-year difference in our ages, many people, Mom included, had trouble telling us apart. Once, we decided to dress alike and confuse folks at our tables. Whenever someone asked one of us for something from the kitchen, we responded, "I'll tell my sister. She's assigned to your table." Much to our delight, it worked.

Aunt Al smiled and shook her head at us, realizing what we were up to. She glanced around the room to make sure everything was in order before heading back to lend a hand in the kitchen. She knew our prank was harmless.

The busy room hummed with eager voices. Rev. Parker welcomed regulars and newcomers

Dede, Polly's look-alike, poses with a mischievous look in her eye.

alike. We placed platters of potato salad trimmed with sprigs of parsley on the tables. We filled water glasses and took orders for coffee or iced tea. When we brought out the steaming bowls of baked beans and baskets of soft rolls, conversation suspended for a short while. Hearty eaters dipped into their second helpings as the clock slowly ticked away.

Dessert consisted of apple, pumpkin, lemon meringue, custard and cherry pies, along with an assortment of cakes. Two, even three helpings of pie and cake made their way to the tables along with refills of coffee.

Finally, those at the tables pushed back their chairs, slipped on their wraps and got up to leave, uttering sincere promises to come again.

With a surge of activity, Polly and I hurried to reset the tables as more people crowded in for their supper. As we delivered more food, a light breeze stirred the tablecloths.

DEDE HAMMOND · ZEPHYRHILLS, FL